GQ

DRIVES

DRIVES

FOREWORD BY
JENSON
BUTTON

GQ

EDITED BY
PAUL HENDERSON

A STYLISH
GUIDE TO THE
GREATEST CARS
EVER MADE

MITCHELL BEAZLEY

Contents

Foreword
Jenson Button

I knew I was lucky. I knew that this wasn't what most kids were getting for Christmas and I knew I couldn't wait to drive it. What I didn't know was 30 years later I'd essentially still be in it. Still grinning, still utterly in love with it to the point of obsession.

It was Christmas Day 1988 and my dad had just presented me with a go-kart. Most kids my age were in their garden kicking around their new football in their new boots – I was staring down at this wondrous machine: the engine, the wheels, the chassis, even the beautifully moulded bucket seat. The funny thing about being given a kart as an eight-year-old is it sounds incredibly lavish. And it was. But my dad didn't buy it for me because he was wealthy, far from it. He bought me that kart because it was all he knew. To him, that was a new ball and a new pair of boots. Whether it was selling cars, building karting engines or racing himself in British rallycross, it was a world he had utterly immersed himself in and one I was completely drawn to and destined to follow him into.

Over the years I would say one of the most common questions I'm asked, to which I still have no answer, is: 'If you hadn't have become a racing driver what would you be?' And I honestly couldn't tell you. I think it frustrates people that I don't have an interesting answer, or an answer at all, but I truly have no clue. That's so unfathomable to me because it's been my life for 31 out of the 39 years I've been around. That kart set me on a journey and ignited a love affair with not just racing, but cars in general. And I've been obsessed ever since.

Aside from those early go-karts and Formula Fords, the first road car I ever drove was the Suzuki 'Jeep' – the square one before the Vitara. My dad would let me drive it in the field across from the house. He remembered looking out the window and seeing me going backwards at 40mph.

The funny thing about competing in karts from such a young age is I had managed to win a few races and championships so had some of my winnings saved up for a car when I finally, famously at the second attempt (everyone knows that story, so I won't bore you), passed my test.

Using £2,000 of my own money, I bought a Vauxhall Cavalier 2.0-litre – the 8V not the 16V (I couldn't afford that) – and it was a dark blue, 1990 G-reg with 90,000 miles on the clock. I put some 17-in wheels on it, Sachs suspension and obviously the speakers every kid had when they were 17.

Actually, that thing drove bloody well, once I was finished with it. It was a good little car.

I then went through a few motors that I didn't actually own; I was given a Ford Cougar for winning the Formula Ford Championship and then a Renault Sport Mégane 2.0 coupé. They were both great fun.

The next car I bought was when I actually got into Formula One. I was 19 years old and I bought a Ferrari. It was a second-hand yellow 355 GTS. It was only two years old and I absolutely loved it. I remember I went to go and view the car at the dealership and wasn't allowed to test-drive it because I wasn't old enough for their insurance, so I had to sit in the passenger seat to get a feel for it. I put the money down, did the paperwork and then drove it home. And I still own that car. I had it in Monaco for a few years. I have so many memories of cruising around the Côte d'Azur in that car that I know I'll definitely keep it forever. That engine is just a beautiful sounding thing, it's like music. I know Dario Franchitti has one with a big loud exhaust on it...so I might do the same.

However, the annoying thing was that in the showroom at the same time, sitting right next to the 355 was an F40. I remember that it was double the price, but still it was only £160,000 for an F40. That car today is worth almost a million pounds.

After the 355 I really got into supercars. I went through a phase of loving the Bugatti Veyron, which I owned for a couple of months. I enjoyed it, but I couldn't deal with the insurance and the servicing. And if you damaged a tyre, it was £5,000 and you had to buy another wheel, which was another £5,000. That wasn't fun. I spent the whole time worrying. So I sold it. Then I bought a Ferrari Enzo...and owned that for all of two weeks. I didn't get on with it at all, it just felt cumbersome and lazy. The problem was it felt like a race car, but wasn't a race car. What exactly was it? Really, I should have held on to it because it would be worth a fortune now.

Then I went through a VW Camper Van phase. Yep, I bought two vans – one for the UK and one for Monaco. One was gold – a 15-window – the other one was originally stickered up and painted as a Coca-Cola van. It had the original 1.2-litre engine in it, so obviously I got rid of that, stuck in a 2.0-litre 200bhp VW engine, did all the suspension, and added Fuchs wheels. I loved that car –

make that love...I still own it as well – and used it for triathlons. We'd get it stickered up with the charity we were raising money for. It became a special car for me, which is why I couldn't get rid of it, even though I haven't driven it (or even seen it) for ten years.

Since moving to LA I'm definitely experiencing a little love affair with American cars, having picked up a 1976 Ford Bronco, a 1956 Chevy Bel Air with a 500hp LS3 engine dropped in, and a 1970 Boss 302 Mustang. Alongside those I also have my 1992 Porsche 964, which I've stripped out and upgraded the suspension/wheels/engine. This is the car I enjoy the canyons with. I've also just taken delivery of a Porsche GT2 RS...which is a monster.

Cars for me, and for a lot of people, are pieces of art. Art that you can play with, that you can touch, listen to or that you can simply stand and admire. And if you are the kind of person that feels the same way, you are really going to enjoy *GQ Drives*. Over the years, British *GQ* have treated their automotive stars no differently to how they capture Hollywood's finest. The lighting, the angle, and the setting are all vitally important in portraying each car in its own individual way.

Some people will never understand what all the 'fuss' is about. Some people will never see past the mere necessity or functionality of a car. For the rest of us, however, we get to marvel in the craftmanship and the beauty of what's already been and wait with bated breath to see what's next.

Jenson Button

Introduction
Paul Henderson

There is a recurring conversation I find myself having at weddings, parties and various social occasions when I meet people for the first time. It goes like this: after the initial politeness and general small talk, sooner or later they will ask me what I do for a living. At first, all I tell them is that I am a journalist and that I work on *GQ*. My new acquaintances are delighted. Magazines are something people know about, right? An easy subject to chat over, a fairly interesting topic, chances are they've probably heard of *GQ*, and they might even be curious about who I have interviewed or stories I may have written. But then comes the inevitable question and that's when it all goes wrong.

'So...' they ask with a smile, 'what areas do you cover?'

'There are three main ones,' I admit, a little sheepishly. 'Firstly, I look after the food and drink section.'

'That's great,' they reply. 'Does that mean you get to meet chefs, visit all the latest restaurants, and drink in new bars?'

I nod.

'Oh, you are making us jealous,' they will say good-naturedly, but their smiles become a little more forced. 'What else do you do?'

Then I tentatively explain that I am also the Sports Editor.

'Seriously?' they ask. I nod again.

'Does that mean you get to go to Wimbledon? The World Cup? The Olympics? Formula One races?' I nod again, and now they can't disguise their envy. 'You are so...lucky.'

At this point someone, usually my wife, in an attempt to change the subject, will interject. 'Well, I'm not really interested in sport. It's just a bit boring, isn't it?'

And for a second, for a fleeting moment, I think maybe I am going to get away with it. But then someone will remember there is a third aspect to my job, and they just have to know. That's when I hit them with the knock-out blow by confessing, as casually as I possibly can, that I am also *GQ*'s Car Editor.

At this point, I guarantee that whomever I am talking to will groan, raise their eyes to the ceiling and say, as light-heartedly as they possibly can (but with impossible-to-suppress bitterness and through gritted teeth), 'God, that's amazing. Good for you.' And then they will walk off, just before they transform into a green-eyed monster of Hulk-like proportions and smash me to pieces.

And the thing is, I can't blame them. I do have something of a dream job, but it is always the cars that upset people. They might not be too bothered about eating in Michelin-star restaurants or fussed to be sitting ringside at an Anthony Joshua fight at Wembley, but getting to drive the fastest, sexiest, coolest, most luxurious cars in the world is something many, many people dream about.

After all, that is why you are reading this book, isn't it? And it's a big reason why people buy *GQ* magazine, because when it comes to the automotive world we take our coverage very seriously. It's why we only use only the finest photographers, recruit the very best journalists, and why we only feature the most interesting and exciting cars that we are truly passionate about.

And of all those cars, the ones you will find within the pages of *GQ Drives,* are the best of the best. Narrowing the selection down to our favourite 50 cars wasn't easy (which is why, if you count them, you'll find there are a few more than that magic number – don't tell the publishers), but to be honest the task ended up being a real labour of love. Choosing our favourite motoring features of the past 15 years was a far tougher assignment than driving the cars in the first place, we can assure you, and we didn't make our choices lightly.

After all, how do you pick your favourite Ferrari? If you are only going to select half-a-dozen classic automotive icons, which ones do you leave out? The British motor industry has been much maligned over the years, and yet we couldn't do a car book without featuring Aston Martin, Bristol or Jaguar. You see, not easy, is it? Not that you should feel too sorry for us.

To help us make up our minds, not only did we revisit our old reviews, but in some cases we felt duty bound to call up the manufacturers of our favourites and ask them to allow us to borrow their cars one more time...just to make sure they were as good as we remembered the first time. (That's the excuse we gave them, anyway.) In our dedication to the content cause you understand, we road tested, then re-road tested, just to be certain we were happy with our list.

And, as you will see, we didn't just confine our assessments to local B-roads and test tracks. Over the years we have driven Bentleys on a tour of the USA, been in search of Romania's best road, dropped off cars by helicopter and travelled everywhere from the Atacama mountains to the streets of Monaco, to ensure we pushed ourselves (and the cars and bikes and boats) to the limit. We even recruited some famous faces along the way to give us a second opinion on our choices – including José Mourinho and Pink Floyd's Nick Mason.

Not only that, but we insisted on only featuring cars that look as good as they drive. Not all the vehicles featured in *GQ Drives* look like they belong in an art gallery, but a lot of them do. And for the ones that aren't quite as photogenic, we made sure to capture them in a setting that brought out their personality. (You might not love the Bentley Bentayga or the Rolls-Royce Cullinan, for example, but they certainly make a statement.) Which is how we managed to pick our final favourites and then parked them all neatly under one roof.

Finally, we asked a world-famous petrolhead, Jenson Button, to write the foreword. A car guy through and through, Jenson not only approved of our list, he actually has owned a fair few of the cars featured within these pages.

The result, hopefully you agree, is pretty spectacular.

And while I am immensely proud of this collection of *GQ*'s greatest hits, just so you know, I am not claiming any of the credit. In this book, the cars are the stars. Which is why, if you do happen to meet me at a wedding or a party, I probably won't rush to tell you that I am the Editor of *GQ Drives*. Believe me, it's not worth the hassle and I don't want you to hate me too.

Paul Henderson

Chapter 1
Italian Stallions

Despite what you may have heard about its beautiful Renaissance art, iconic architecture and stunning countryside, Italy is only really famous for three things: pizza, pasta and horsepower. And of those three, we are only interested in the one that feeds the soul. Italian supercars may lack the sophistication and ultra-efficient engineering of some countries' production cars (*ja,* we're talking about you, Germany), but they make up for it in passion, power and pure heart-racing performance. The appeal of these jet fighters on wheels, be they Ferrari, Lamborghini or Maserati (they don't all have to end in an 'i', but it certainly helps), may have started in prepubescence with the Hot Wheels toy box or posters on the bedroom wall, but it never really stops – especially if you are lucky enough to slide into one of those awkward driving seats, fire up that Black Sabbath sound-test engine and put your foot ever so slightly on the accelerator. If you ever get to that point, lust turns to love and you will be hooked forever. To drive an Italian supercar...that's *amore.*

Lamborghini Huracán
The balance of power

The Lamborghini Huracán's virtual cockpit and angular curves made the marque as alpha as ever – but the user-friendly controls meant the ride could have lost its edge.

The world of fuel-guzzling internal combustion is still under attack. Industrial-scale navel-gazing has seen all-electric start-up Tesla go from zero to Nasdaq hero in no time at all, while BMW has gambled in excess of £2 billion ($3.3 billion) on its ultra-efficient i3 and i8 uber-brands. Even Ferrari has succumbed to the hybrid buzz, on its £1.1 million ($1.4 million) V12 LaFerrari hypercar, and turbo-charging elsewhere in its range. It's also known as 'forced induction', and some of Maranello's finest admit that EU legislation has pretty much forced them to do it. It's the best way to preserve performance while cleaning up emissions and reducing consumption, but it can chisel away at the emotion.

So where now for the hairy-chested, macho-man sports car? Lamborghini has long been the poster boy for well-heeled automotive playboys, as priapic as Andy Warhol's celebrated art for the Stones' *Sticky Fingers* album. Not for nothing did Martin Scorsese cast a Countach as the literal and metaphorical vehicle for Leonardo DiCaprio's spectacular Quaalude comedown in *The Wolf of Wall Street* (2014).

On the face of it, the new Lamborghini Huracán is as cocksure as ever. There's the name for a start, a legendary 19th-century fighting bull from Alicante, or the Mayan god of wind, storm and fire – both are prototypical. The company's chief designer, Filippo Perini, once compared the planes and geometry of the bigger Lamborghini Aventador to Jean-Paul Goude's work with Grace Jones in the early Eighties – an inspired reference point that suggests a deliciously broad world view. Some online snipers dismissed the Huracán as too safe, but in the flesh it's a truly artful mix of curves and angles, and introduces a welcome maturity after the increasingly extreme Sesto Elemento, Veneno and Egoista.

The interior is even better. Lamborghini has a technical partnership with Boeing and has long invoked fighter jets as inspiration. This is now undeniable. Gone are the analogue instruments of old. Gone, too, is the central multimedia screen. Instead, the Huracán has a brilliant 12.3in TFT 'virtual cockpit' in the main binnacle that can be configured to show an enlarged rev counter and speed readout, a satnav display, an audio feed or a mix of them all.

Firing up the Huracán is pure Hollywood. The start button sits under a red flap that you flick up, as if priming a missile, but instead prompting a brusque

ENGINE
5,204cc, direct injection
V10, 602bhp
PERFORMANCE
0–62mph in 3.2 secs;
top speed 202mph
YEAR OF RELEASE
2014
PRICE ON RELEASE
£180,720 ($241,995)

starter-motor whir before the cylinders erupt. There are ten of them behind your head, and an enamelled badge on the engine block even outlines the *ordine di ascensione* (firing order). The engine is a 5.2-litre unit, a heavily reworked version of the one that powered the Huracán's predecessor, the Gallardo (Lambo's most successful car ever, with more than 14,000 sold). It has forged pistons, an aluminium silicon crank and a clever new exhaust system.

It's usually wise to ease yourself into an unknown supercar. Lamborghini's Nineties Diablo was aptly named and routinely caught out the unwary. But the Huracán's user-friendliness is immediately apparent. Three things define it. First, it uses a new dual-clutch seven-speed gearbox – there is no longer a manual option – which slurs with buttery smoothness through the gears in auto mode and is just as good with the steering-column-mounted flappy paddles. Then there is its ride quality, which remains composed and unruffled, even on seriously broken blacktop. Finally, the Huracán has a four-wheel-drive chassis and brilliantly accurate electromechanical power steering, and its body – which uses a mix of carbonfibre reinforced plastic (CFRP) and aluminium – has fantastic torsional properties. So even just chuntering along on the motorway, this Lamborghini imparts a sense of indomitability. The most alpha and masculine of car brands has seemingly wised up. But is that really what we want?

Tellingly, the 'Anima' button on the steering wheel (Adaptive Network Intelligent Management) allows the driver to choose between 'Strada', 'Sport' or 'Corsa' modes, remapping the car's ingenious chassis electronics, suspension settings and throttle response. However, that might not be quite enough for some. This is an awesome car, one that beams itself like a physics-defying time machine between corners without relinquishing its grip. But it also approaches the business of high performance rather like Robocop approaches law enforcement – failing to see that pure driving entertainment lies as much on the empirically unquantifiable edges as it does in the middle, no matter how accomplished it may be.

Who would have thought it? A Lamborghini that is almost too good.

Ferrari 458 Italia
Dark side of the vroom

Pink Floyd legend and supercar aficionado Nick Mason swapped drum stool for driver's seat and found that Ferrari's 458 Italia blurred the lines between road and racetrack more than ever. It rocks.

ENGINE
4.5-litre V8, 562bhp
PERFORMANCE
0–62mph in 3.4 secs;
top speed 202mph
YEAR OF RELEASE
2009
PRICE ON RELEASE
£170,000 ($227,625)

Ah, yes. The Ferrari 458. It's red and it's got lots of switches, knobs and buttons. The trouble is that any sort of test of this car requires a lot of time, not only in the driver's seat driving, but also with the car stationary and with a race-engineer nerd to explain all the available settings. Obviously, as a real man, this was completely out of the question...instructions are for amateurs. And, to be perfectly honest, I assumed that with some Enzo experience, as well as familiarity with the new California, it would all become crystal clear. Sadly, this was a mistaken assumption.

The reality, and perhaps one of this car's finest qualities, is that the 458 is really easy to use at a basic level. For starters, unlike so many supercars, you can actually see out of it. This may sound a little obvious, but all too often it seems that the manufacturers of some of these wonder machines assume you have a man with a red flag walking in front to clear the way. Sometimes these supercars seem to be the development platforms for the production cars, with the customers acting as test drivers. Actually, Ferrari has done this officially with the FXX Enzo, where the data taken from track-day testing by customers was downloaded to the factory race department. I'm not sure if much was learned from the privateers struggling to get to grips with 700-odd brake horsepower, but I think everyone enjoyed the experience. And, inevitably, some of that research must have found its way to the 458. Apparently, the 458 in Challenge form is only two seconds a lap slower than the FXX...

I digress. What the 458 does is allow the serious driver to set the car up to his or her personal requirements according to the road conditions and the type of driving anticipated. The big news here is that even with a wannabe racing driver at the wheel, it's going to be faster on a circuit with the traction control engaged rather than switched off. In this respect, the car is (almost) foolproof, and all the more magical for that. There was a time when traction control was used to slow the car down as soon as events became exciting, to ensure adhesion to the road. Now it simply enables the driver to press on far beyond that and power the car through a corner, even in the wet, with the only drama being the loud squeal of tyres and passenger.

Bear in mind, though, it's still a matter of degrees. Even on the softest setting it's unlikely to threaten a Rolls-Royce in the comfort stakes, but then the Ferrari is likely to finish a lap of the Nürburgring Nordschleife so far ahead that there will be time to get the best table in the nearby Pistenklause

restaurant and have eaten its speciality of pig's trotters by the time the Roller arrives. I know this because I once took a Phantom around the 174-corner, 13-mile track, and it's perfectly capable of turning in a respectable lap time if pressed, but it's still only going to finish in time for the coffee and mints.

For those interested in the technical specifications, slip on your geek glasses and we'll begin. A 4,499cc, V8 engine powers the 458 Italia, producing 562bhp at a maximum of 9,000 rpm with direct fuel injection. Transmission is a Getrag dual-clutch, seven-speed unit, similar to the California. Suspension is double wishbones at the front and a multi-link setup at the rear, coupled with E-diff and F1-Trac traction control systems. ABS CCM brakes ensure that 62–0mph braking distance is down to 32.5m (107ft). The magnetorheological dampers (have you lost the will to live yet?) were codeveloped with Delphi, and the car is fitted with Bridgestone Potenza S001 tyres. Surely that's enough?

No? Ferrari's official acceleration figure is 0–62mph in 3.4 seconds, while the top speed is more than 202mph. And I can't believe you want the fuel and downforce figures as well...

Perhaps the most important part of the story is that the car looks stunning. The body was designed by Pininfarina, as with all recent Ferrari models. It really is one of the most elegant cars to come out of Maranello, and the simplicity of the shape is in many ways a return to earlier principles after the extremes of the Enzo. The interior is both spacious and practical. So it should be, as seven times Formula One world champion Michael Schumacher was involved in the design, and the steering wheel is the closest yet to the one you see on a Formula One car, with almost all the required controls fitted on it. And if you haven't been leaning over a Formula One car recently, I can tell you it bears a startling resemblance to the one you see on the screen of your favourite driving video game. But you may wish to stick to the games console when you hear the pricing. The list price is £170,000 ($227,625), and that's before adding on an iPod connector weighing in at £540 ($881), the tip of the iceberg of good accessories you would probably want. The future for this sort of car is an ever-increasing list of options to enable you to create your very own vehicle.

And what of the opposition? The good news is that this is the best Ferrari yet, and you don't have to go scrabbling round a shady dealership to try to pick up that old classic. But there are plenty of contenders anxious to climb into the ring. Porsche has the 911 GT2 RS, but it does it all in an older-fashioned way. There's the Audi R8, with a four-wheel-drive transmission system that's frankly the most sophisticated out there, but it's slower at the top end (196mph). Then there's the Mercedes SLS AMG: you see it working as the safety car at grand prix races, which must mean something. It's a lot cruder than the 458, and is probably most suited to a sportsman with more money than sense.

For double the money there's the Lexus LFA. All carbon-fibre body and chassis, it uses a 4.8-litre V10, has a sci-fi appearance and is limited to 500, which bodes well for residuals. The Noble is also not cheap (a rather startling £200,000-odd/$292,000) but it is adored by all who've driven it. The Lamborghini Gallardo Superleggera is a little outdated technically, but it still looks as outrageous as a Lamborghini should. And if you must buy British, there's the Aston Martin DBS, which looks fantastic and has a tailored, modern British feel inside but is a real modern muscle car. Finally, there's the dark horse, the McLaren MP4-12C, which is intended to go head-to-head with the 458. The MP4-12C has a clever carbon-fibre monocoque chassis and a highly sophisticated 3.8-litre, 600bhp twin turbo. The chassis and electronics are F1-derived and the interior seemingly wraps around the driver.

Probably the most difficult question to answer about the 458 is whether to have its seats monogrammed or accept that you will want to sell it one day. And there may be a problem in limiting your potential buyer to someone with similar initials. I leave it to you to decide who gets the driver's seat.

Alfa Romeo 4C
Alfa and omega

Alfa Romeo's 4C was both the embodiment of Italian automotive sex appeal and a vision of the future.

ENGINE
1.75-litre, 4-cylinder turbo, 240bhp
PERFORMANCE
0–62mph in 4.5 secs; top speed 160mph
YEAR OF RELEASE
2013
PRICE ON RELEASE
£45,000 ($55,195)

There's a revealing moment in Ron Howard's 2013 motor-racing epic *Rush*, in which James Hunt's patron Lord Hesketh proclaims to the great man's latest conquest, 'Men love women. But even more than that, men love cars.' It's true. And when it comes to Italian cars, that appreciation acquires an almost febrile intensity. The likes of Ferrari, Lamborghini and Pagani long ago figured out how to commingle art, machinery, performance and pornography, in a way that their more prosaic British and German rivals simply never have. Look back further and even basic Italian cars have a charm that transcends their proletarian roots.

When *Top Gear* magazine named its sexiest car of all time, it wasn't a Ferrari but the original Fiat 500 that won out. Alfa Romeo sits somewhere in between. No mainstream car company has ever created so many beautiful vehicles or loaded the ownership experience with so much pleasure and pain. The new 4C certainly serves up its fair share of visual entertainment but, more important, it runs with an engineering philosophy that is fast gaining traction: downsizing. The 4C's dry weight is an impressively light 895kg (1 tonne), so while it's powered by a relatively weedy-sounding 1.75-litre, four-cylinder engine, its 240bhp is enough to give this little Alfa Romeo a proper supercar-busting power-to-weight ratio (268bhp per tonne, since you ask). And that, as anyone who really understands cars knows, is a far more accurate performance barometer than the fabled but rather meaningless 0–62mph sprint.

It also packs a huge amount of high technology into its lissom form. The big selling point is the 4C's 'pre-preg' carbon chassis: light, strong and extremely rigid. With annual volumes of 3,500 cars, this Alfa could represent the tipping point for an exotic technology that's previously been the preserve of vastly more expensive supercars and a mainstay of Formula One. Such is the Byzantine nature of the modern car business, the 4C is actually handmade at Maserati's plant in Modena, where its 864 separate components have to pass 351 different tests, and men with clipboards talk about the 'annihilation of defects'. Which country are we in again?

'There is simply nothing else on the market as innovative or that uses this technology that is available at this price,' the former Alfa Romeo brand boss Louis-Carl Vignon told me. 'This is a laboratory car for us, and there is no doubt that we will see an extension of what we learn here in other Alfa Romeos. I respect the Bugatti Veyron, but I doubt that a Veyron driver would

be able to keep pace with the 4C on a good mountain road.' Well, mountain roads don't come much better than the one that carves its way improbably up the Colle del Nivolet in the Italian Alps. This is where Michael Caine and the lads were left with a precipitous pile of Mafia gold in *The Italian Job* (1969) and it's the sort of demanding tarmac ribbon the 4C could have been custom-made for.

Yet again, though, Alfa Romeo has created a car that flatters to deceive. Its chassis is terrific, thankfully, and because it has unassisted steering and relatively skinny front tyres, it dives in and out of corners with astonishing tenacity. Italian race-car brake supplier Brembo has provided the 4C's stoppers, and they're full of feel. In other words, this is a car that positively fizzes in your hands.

Unfortunately, it also pops, bangs and chirrups in your ears. Fitting a four-cylinder engine is a compromise and the 4C's turbo-charged unit isn't a match for the rest of the car. Lower the windows and find a tunnel and the 4C sounds like a Sixties racing car, especially if it's fitted with the optional sports exhaust. Inside, though, it settles into a rather strident drone. Forced induction also generates lag, and the 4C needs to be kept firmly in the zone to do its best work. Its dual-clutch paddle-shift can be irritatingly inconsistent, too.

But how much does that matter? What we have here is an eye-poppingly pretty £45,000 ($55,195) Alfa Romeo underpinned by the same sci-fi technology that McLaren will charge you £200,000 ($230,00) for. It goes like hell, but returns an average of 41mpg. It sticks decades of Italian automotive sex appeal in a blender and gives it a futuristic twist. Just remember that a degree of masochism still comes as standard.

Ferrari FF
The fourth dimension

When Ferrari's first ever four-wheel drive finally touched down, it took prancing horsepower to new heights.

ENGINE
6.3-litre V12, 651bhp
PERFORMANCE
0–62mph in 3.7 secs;
top speed 208mph
YEAR OF RELEASE
2011
PRICE ON RELEASE
£227,026 ($298,750)

A Ferrari estate? You could say that. Our Continental colleagues prefer the more evocative term 'shooting brake', which conjures up images of pheasant shooting or perhaps a spot of gran turismo Euro action to a chateau. It's a slightly odd-looking thing, the FF, but an indisputably more stylish way to travel than by low-budget airline.

Not that there aren't earlier fastback incarnations. There are various special editions lurking in Ferrari's back catalogue, including the compelling 250 GTO 'Breadvan' commissioned by an Italian count in 1962 for racing; a bizarre Daytona by Brit oddball Panther; and a 456 estate created for Prince Jefri of Brunei. And there's also a philosophical similarity to unsung British heroes such as the Reliant Scimitar or Jensen FF, to which the new Ferrari owes a bigger debt than just its name.

Resurrecting the rather arcane styling tropes of the fast estate actually makes perfect sense. Ferrari would never admit it, but this car exists because, gulp, market research suggests that this is what customers at this oxygen-thin end of the automotive stratosphere actually want. A V12 Ferrari with continent-crushing performance, room inside for four well-heeled adults, enough boot space for their luggage and all-wheel drive for the first time ever in a Ferrari. A car for all road conditions, then. Or, less charitably, a four-wheel drive Ferrari estate.

But, boy, does it work. The FF is, in all senses, pure Ferrari GT: 6.3-litre, 651bhp V12 mounted up front and cradled in a (relatively) lightweight aluminium chassis, seven-speed dual-clutch gearbox connected to a rear transaxle with a clever electronic differential. All sublime on a perfectly dry road, but liable to be a bit tricky when the roads turn slippery. Or snowy. When did you ever see a car like this being driven on snow? It's precisely why Ferrari had the Italian army air drop a pair of FFs 2,300m (7,500ft) up a ski slope in the southern Tyrol and let *GQ* loose.

Now, 651bhp and compacted snow are usually a recipe for disaster, but the hardware under that elongated body is so clever it's initially disorienting. The FF does things that nothing with comparable power and performance could ever dream of pulling off. How? Well, the issue with conventional four-wheel drives is that the extra drive shaft adds a load of weight, blunts the way the car turns into a corner and generally interferes with its handling balance.

The FF doesn't mess with your fun, it amplifies it by using what Ferrari calls a 'power transfer unit' (PTU). This lightweight box of tricks (just 40kg/88lb) contains a set of helical-cut gears and a pair of continuously slipping wet clutches that, along with a legion of electronics, sends torque to the front wheels when the PTU figures you need it. It can even tell in advance how much grip you're likely to need as you brake into a corner and power through it. On a dry road, depending on whether you've flicked the steering wheel-mounted manettino chassis control to 'comfort', 'sport' or 'ESC off' (effectively 'race' mode), this is maximum attack Ferrari. The bizarre thing about the FF is that it's still maximum attack Ferrari even if there's a blizzard blowing outside your front door. With the 'snow & ice' setting engaged, it's like having a shrunken, invisible Fernando Alonso intervening when you run out of talent.

This leaves you free to enjoy the spectral wail of that incredible V12 engine hitting its 8,200rpm peak like some portable industrial mill, to surf up and down through a paddle-shift transmission that swaps gears with buttery smoothness, to travel very, very fast indeed (208mph, if you fancy; 62mph in 3.7 seconds), before leaning on a set of carbon-ceramic brakes, which, though lacking feel at the top of the pedal, still stop you with brick-wall finality.

The interior is the most opulent Ferrari has ever created, even if its basic architecture could be more flamboyant. Front-seat passengers also get their own digital readout, which shows how hard the front wheels are working, gearshifts and speed. In a car like the FF, I think I'd prefer not to know. It seems that, even at £227,000 ($298,750), before options, the FF isn't just the most versatile Ferrari ever, it's also the most egalitarian.

Lamborghini Gallardo
Sex machine

Certain men used to think that the car they drove said as much about their 'masculinity' as it did about their taste in motors. But Lamborghini's Gallardo had a pulling power all of its own...

I'm not going to lie – testing cars for a living has plenty to recommend it. You get first go in everything from hot hatches to hypercars, often in glamorous or exotic settings, and you can pretend that the car you are in is yours, all yours. In fact, slipping in and out of different motors is a bit like acting – you're not just driving, you're inhabiting a different skin.

And the response you get from spectators is often illuminating. For example, a woman in an old Range Rover made a rude gesture at me once as I rounded a corner at some speed in a BMW Z4. I suspect it would have been different if I'd been driving a Saab or an Audi (but then, so would the corner). Estates and MPVs may communicate your reliability, but perhaps at the expense of any measure of adventurousness. And the frugal supermini suggests either you care too much or you don't care enough. It's a minefield out there.

Until a supercar enters the equation. The term was coined 30-odd years ago to describe the new breed of extreme sports cars then gathering momentum as an industry force. Ideally, the supercar's engine would sit in the middle, feature 12 cylinders and be clothed in a body that exploded into view with all the understatement of Bianca Jagger sitting astride a stallion in the middle of Studio 54's dance floor. Of all the contenders at the time, and with the profanely named Countach in particular, Lamborghini did it best.

It still does. Which isn't to say that owning one is your gateway to endless erotic attention. Far from it. True enough that in bright yellow – *giallo bolognese* – the new Gallardo positively invites comment and certainly isn't the place for a furtive nose rummage or illegal phone conversation, never mind anything more stimulating. The bigger problem is that most people tend to think roughly the same thing about Lamborghini drivers. And as I drove down London's Regent Street in the Gallardo you see here, one bystander decided to vent her spleen. 'Oh look at me in my fantastic yellow car,' she hissed. 'I've got a really tiny penis.'

The Gallardo is the latest in a long line of visual spectaculars about which onlookers are inclined to make such vituperative assessments. But, wild as it might appear, deep down this is as thoughtful a car as Lamborghini has managed since its impressive debut with the 1963 350GT. Gone, for example, are the 'scissors' doors, which have long been a Lambo highlight. Getting into the Gallardo is relatively easy but, because it's still so ludicrously low,

ENGINE
5.0-litre quad-cam V10, 500bhp
PERFORMANCE
0–62mph in 4.2 secs; top speed 193mph
YEAR OF RELEASE
2003
PRICE ON RELEASE
£117,000 ($167,200)

it's hardly the car for weekly visits to the osteopath. Vision is also limited, and with its swollen hips it's a real challenge to reverse park. Plus, the alloy wheels are so huge and expensive, every kerb offers the potential for costly embarrassment. And the lack of ground clearance at the front means speed humps should be met with caution or, preferably, in a different car altogether.

Then there's the interior. Lambos of old had switchgear so randomly arranged that the radio came on when you wanted the wipers, and ventilation controls could only be reached when the gear lever was in reverse and you had the body of an orang-utan. Not terribly handy when doing 100mph in a tropical downpour. Now the company is owned by Audi, the Gallardo's cabin is exquisitely put together, it smells wonderful and works with fearsome logic; the only exception is the headlight switch, nestled invisibly in a row of identical switches.

Just as you begin thinking, 'Hmm, big sporty Audi, could be a bit dull,' you fire up the engine and its ten cylinders begin an impatient stampede not five inches behind your left ear. Nothing propelled by a 500bhp, 5.0-litre, quad-cam V10 is going to be dull, and the moment you unleash the whole savage lot you stop worrying about getting to the osteopath and, above all else, what size the world thinks your penis is.

This is a glorious motor car. From just 1,500rpm, the Lamborghini's variable valve timing and variable intake geometry ensure power is shovelled onto the road (via all four wheels) in a gigantic, smooth surge. Between 3,500 and 7,000rpm it's working at maximum efficiency. At 7,800rpm, all 500bhp are busy, giving the driver something to really chew on while approaching scenery-straining warp speed. Yet the Gallardo remains supremely well planted throughout, due to its fully flat underbody and clever design. Lamborghinis have rarely been all that efficient, but at 190mph-plus, it's good to know they are now.

In its own way then, it is reliable, efficient and fun. Maybe that's not such a bad impression to give after all...

Maserati MC12
The best car *GQ* had ever driven (back then!)

What made GQ *fall in love with the Maserati MC12?*

ENGINE
6.0-litre V12, 621bhp

PERFORMANCE
0–62mph in 3.8 secs;
top speed 205mph

YEAR OF RELEASE
2004

PRICE ON RELEASE
£408,000 ($792,000)

Normally I'd bury the cold, hard facts in the middle of my column somewhere and lure you in with a bit of colourful back story or maybe a fragrant anecdote or two. This time, though, I'm going to lay the heavy stuff on you right away.

This is the Maserati MC12. No more than 55 will ever be made. Each one costs around £400,000 ($800,000). It is powered by a 6.0-litre V12 engine, mid-mounted and primed to deliver 621bhp at 7,500rpm. Its top speed is 205mph, and it will accelerate to 62mph in 3.8 seconds. It has a six-speed transmission, over which the driver has control via a paddle-shift sequential manual gearbox. And, in response to the one question I'm asked more often than 'How much money do you think Jeremy Clarkson earns in a year?', the answer is this: 'The best car I have ever driven is the Maserati MC12.'

Which is something of a relief, to be honest. Because this isn't the first time the MC12 has graced the pages of *GQ*, and in citing it as one of the '100 best things in the world right now' (*GQ*, December 2004), we may have been guilty of, how can I put this, a little journalistic licence. Because the truth was we hadn't actually *driven* it when we opted to include it. Frankly, we just liked the cut of its jib. The fact is that until early 2005, nobody outside Maserati's four walls had even so much as sat in an MC12. Very few people ever will. The important thing, however, is that we can now count ourselves among the lucky ones. We've sat in it. And driven it. Around the full Silverstone Grand Prix circuit, and we weren't hanging about. Which means that we can now confirm what we suspected all along. The Maserati isn't just one of the 100 best things in the world, it's one of the best ever.

For a start, there's its wild appearance. When I was a kid I doodled shapes like this all over my school books. Hell, I'm still doodling shapes like this when I should be paying attention in important marketing meetings. I'm not the only one: ask any proper car designer and they'll tell you it's the juvenilia lurking at the back of their minds that they really want to let rip with, not the blueprint for the interior door handles on the next generation mini-MPV.

Well, somebody certainly enjoyed himself on the MC12. Giorgetto Giugiaro, actually, a figure as talismanic and influential in the world of car design as Giorgio Armani is in fashion. The parallels don't end there; as with clothes and music, the influence of previous eras blows across the years, and the MC12's body is a wildly evocative conflation of Seventies and Eighties curves, muscle

and caricature. If it looks like a racing car, then that's because it is: already successfully contesting the FIA GT championship, the rules require that 25 MC12s be 'homologated' for road use. (Homologation is one of the more arcane motor-racing rules, but also one of my favourites, because it means we get cars like this legally, if a little comically, trying to weave their way through congested traffic.)

It's also worth noting that the Maserati – remember the company was taken over by Ferrari in 1997 – is a heavily reworked race version of its Enzo stablemate, so it shares the same incredible carbon-fibre chassis, engine and suspension layout. If anything, though, it's the MC12 that's the more eye-popping: shark-nosed, bewinged, so scooped, slatted and slashed that your inner child performs somersaults every time he claps eyes on it. Yet it still flows better than the aggressively aerodynamic Enzo.

The race-car genealogy is also apparent when you climb inside. A huge slab of bodywork detaches itself as you open the door; in fact, the door *is* a slab of bodywork. Those in the know will recognize the provenance of the carbon fibre and leather that decorate the interior, and they'll enjoy clamping themselves into the seat with a race-spec harness. There's no carpet. Those who know nothing will find little in the way of gadgetry to play with, and a functionally plain dash layout. There are air vents, air con, Maserati's signature analogue clock and not a lot else. Even the rear-view mirror is redundant: there's no window behind your head, just a black panel, giving rise to a creeping claustrophobia. It's all good. And then you spot the starter button, and the 'race' switch, which stiffens the dampers, sharpens throttle response and abbreviates gearshift times. Better still.

Before the MC12 can unleash the full fury of its V12, though, it has a few further surprises to unleash first. There might be beautifully designed mechanical mayhem going on 15 inches away from your head but the beast is surprisingly cultured – at tick-over anyway. It feels oddly comfortable. And engaging first gear and pulling away isn't the customary nerve-shredding, juddering race-car nightmare. It's *easy*.

The MC12 is also very long and very wide, but while I wouldn't want to parallel park it in central London, the Maserati soon folds itself into you, like a great sports car should. All its controls have a delicious tactility, a perfect

weighting. The carbon-fibre steering wheel is thin but feeds back fat gobbets of information from the road surface. The fear – someone else's half a million pound car, a damp, empty racetrack – subsides remarkably quickly.

Silverstone has many tricky corners, and many ways to dump a 600bhp-plus supercar into the scenery. But the Maserati has to be just about the most forgiving mid-engined supercar I've ever driven. I commit several schoolboy errors – trailing throttle into a very fast fifth-gear corner, a dab of the brakes in the middle of another one – yet we sail on oblivious rather than into oblivion. There's a surprising compliance from the suspension, too, an overall lack of aggression. Even if you know what you're doing, the MC12 gives you the confidence to go beyond.

Then, as we pull 150mph or more down Hangar Straight and into Stowe Corner, I remember that it was here that Michael Schumacher slammed into a tyre barrier during the 1999 British Grand Prix and broke his leg. Another cold, hard fact pops into my head: time to stop before I run out of talent.

Chapter 2
German Heavyweights

The automotive slogans that come straight out of Deutschland tell their own story. From Audi's 'advancement through technology' and Mercedes-Benz's 'the best or nothing', right through to BMW's 'designed for driving pleasure', you know what to expect from the best German manufacturers: four-wheeled perfection. Delivering impeccable style, brilliant engineering and next-level technological innovation, whatever you think you might want from a new car, chances are that the Germans have already come up with the idea, optimized the system, wrapped it up in a super-sleek package and are watching it roll off the production line before you've even articulated it. And they really can do it all. Four-door, ferociously fast saloons? You've got it. Luxurious tech-laden limos? *Kein Problem.* Mid-engined plug-in hybrid, face-melting, groin-tingling hypercars? Step right this way.

It seems apt then to borrow what is perhaps one of the most famous car slogans ever, created by Porsche in the Eighties, to define this next chapter. Because when it comes to German automotive engineering...there is no substitute.

Porsche 918 Spyder
Along came a spyder…

With a top speed of 214mph and five driving modes, the Porsche 918 hypercar certainly had bite.

ENGINE
4.6-litre V8 hybrid, 876bhp
PERFORMANCE
0–62mph in 2.5 secs;
top speed 214mph
YEAR OF RELEASE
2013
PRICE ON RELEASE
£715,000 ($847,975)

There are various ways of working out how fast a car really is. Most obviously, there's the stopwatch, against which Porsche's new £715,000 ($847,975) 918 Spyder is little short of ballistic. It'll do 62mph in 2.5 seconds, 124mph in 7.2, 186mph in less than 20, and 214mph flat out. In all the key increments, it'll search out the Bugatti Veyron and dismantle its claim to 'world's fastest' status with pathological attention to detail.

Then there's the Nürburgring circuit. Now firmly established as the definitive testing – and marketing – battleground for the big players, the 918 has nailed a lap of this near-14-mile pressure cooker in 6 minutes 57 seconds. That's an almost cosmically fast time for what is, when all's said and done, a road car. And Porsche reckons it can go faster still.

But you know you're in a car liberally sprinkled with next-level genius when even the company test driver struggles to get away from you. Especially when the driver in question is the legendary Walter Röhrl, a former double world rally champion. Yet even armed with a weapons-grade Porsche 911 Turbo S, Röhrl can't shake off the 918 as we follow him down the main straight of the Ricardo Tormo MotoGP circuit near Valencia. Through the fast corners he has the 911 visibly dancing on the limit, where the 918 remains well within itself. Extraordinary.

It's hard not to come over hyperbolic about this new Porsche hypercar. It arrives at the same time as McLaren's P1 and Ferrari's ludicrously named but otherwise mind-blowing LaFerrari. All three can lay claim to changing the game, and there are intriguing philosophical differences that delineate roughly along German, British and Italian lines. Most significantly, all three are hybrids, at a stroke permitting that oft-maligned 'green' technology to slough off its Prius piety and show what it can do to enhance performance, as well as reduce emissions. Well, it's about time.

Porsche has taken the last part of the equation further than its rivals: in the 918, the driver can choose from five different modes, ingeniously tapping into the car's race-bred 4.6-litre, 599bhp, V8 plus two electric motors – worth around another 277bhp combined – in a variety of ways. This is how we found ourselves in the midst of a multimillion-pound convoy, tripping silently on zero-emission pure electric power only, through Santiago Calatrava and Félix Candela's suitably trippy City of Arts and Sciences in Valencia.

The 918 can do this for around 25 miles, an unimpeachably cool party trick that also allows Porsche to claim an average fuel economy figure of 94mpg and emissions of 70g/km. Not even the saintliest of drivers will ever get near that in reality, but it'll still do 30mpg, even when you're really going for it. And that really is astonishing in the context of its sky-scraping performance.

Despite the all-electric cleverness, however, the 918 remains a fabulous advertisement for internal combustion. Based on the unit in Porsche's RS Spyder endurance racer, its 4.6-litre V8 makes a nape-tingling noise. It's hooked up to an electric motor that sends a mountainous amount of torque to the rear wheels, the electric bit doing its thing at low revs before the petrol engine comes on song further up the rev range. The second electric motor acts on the front axle, to provide additional traction and effectively turning the 918 into an all-wheel-drive car, while even more electronics distribute all this power and energy to the wheels that need it most.

It sounds and is furiously complicated, but at no point on a hot lap – and there's a red button on the wheel that sets you up for exactly that – does any of it obscure the messages passed to your hands. The 918's steering and chassis responses are linear and confidence-inspiring, the gear changes on its PDK dual-shift 'box eye-blink fast, and the whole thing manages to be genuinely electrifying without straining every sinew the driver has, as was so often the way with mid-engined supercars.

Porsche has also gone to the trouble of reimagining its interior multimedia telematics, and the 918's controls are arranged in an Ive-esque touchscreen bridge. It's an easy car to see out of and use, and magnificently well made, all of which lends itself to a remarkably Zen-like driving experience in full-electric mode.

Kick-start that V8, though, and the 918 transcends everything you thought you knew about high-performance cars. Truly, there has never been anything quite like it.

Audi R8
The artful eight

From the racetrack to Hollywood, the game-changing Audi R8 was the everyday supercar that continued to set the standards ten years after it revved onto our roads.

ENGINE
5.2-litre V10 Plus, 602bhp
PERFORMANCE
0–62mph in 3.2 secs;
top speed 205mph
YEAR OF RELEASE
2016 (second generation)
PRICE ON RELEASE
£135,000 ($192,450)

Trailed by 2003's visionary Le Mans concept and a starring role in the Will Smith movie *I, Robot* (2004), Audi's 21st-century rebirth reached a zenith for me personally on a road roughly an hour's drive outside Las Vegas. Sin City's neon was a glitzy sideshow to a car that was instantly as brilliant as anything Audi had ever previously magicked up. Red Rock Canyon looked great that day; the rust-coloured landscape serving up the kinds of road America isn't supposed to be any good at: fast and undulating, decent but not overlong straights punctuated with sweeping fourth-gear corners and trickier hairpins. Billiard-table-smooth surfaces intermingled with tarmac that wouldn't have passed muster on the moon. Only the best could survive this sort of test – and the R8 was mighty.

At one point we were airborne over a crest, yet the R8's expertly calibrated suspension just shrugged it off. The all-new mid-engined Audi supercar might have looked like a showbiz spaceship, but as well as a paddle-shifting semi-auto – the new orthodoxy – it was also available with an old-fashioned six-speed manual gearbox. And a while later, the V10 version arrived.

Maybe it shouldn't have been that much of a surprise. Back in 2007, Audi was midway through a domination of endurance racing, Le Mans 24 Hours in particular, that motorsport titans like Ferrari may never match (nine wins, the last in 1965), and was challenging even Porsche's tally (to date, 19 plays 13).

'Le Mans remains a laboratory that is ideal for developing new technologies,' Audi's former head of motorsport Dr Wolfgang Ullrich told me. 'The relevance for production cars is always of great importance for us.' Success at the top level of endurance racing wasn't the only impetus for the original R8, although it was the most conspicuous. Audi knew it had work to do on its driver appeal, too. Despite a history stretching back to the fearsome Auto Union Grand Prix cars that dominated motorsport in the Thirties (engineered by one Ferdinand Porsche before he launched his own company) and the arrival of the all-wheel-drive quattro coupé in 1980 (developed by Porsche's grandson and future Volkswagen Group chief Ferdinand Piëch), Audi's reputation for driving entertainment had wobbled. Beautifully engineered and better built than any other brand, yes, but saddled with narcotic steering and leaden chassis dynamics.

'The R8 represented a significant step-change for the company,' said Roland Schala, Head of Project Management for the Audi R8. 'It was our first super sports car with quattro and a mid-engined layout. It had the task to increase the sportiness and prestige of the Audi brand. A memorable moment occurred the first time we presented the R8 at a dynamic test drive to our board of management – that was an important milestone for us. The R8 project really started to grow – prior to this it was a small project with a small number of people working on it.'

After that, the R8's mission was demanding but clearly delineated. 'Our cars are never brazen in their styling but neither do they deny their performance potential,' Schala continued. 'Audi occupies a unique position, more than ever before. With the R8 we have continued to sharpen our profile with the aim of giving the Audi brand an even more progressive character.'

In 2016, the sharpening and shapeshifting have become sharper still. That DIY gearbox has gone, as has the 'entry-level' 4.2-litre V8. The choice now is between two versions of the excellent 5.2-litre V10, the lesser of which runs a mere 533bhp, while the V10 Plus makes 602bhp at a thrilling 8,250rpm. That equates to a top speed of 205mph, and a 0–62mph time of 3.2 seconds, making it the fastest road-going Audi ever. In fact, there aren't many cars that can break the double-tonne, so the R8 V10 Plus now takes its place alongside a perma-vaping Leo DiCaprio and Léa Seydoux in the VIP inner circle of your dreams. Meanwhile, rival 'everyday supercar' manufacturers will be having nothing but nightmares.

Proper respect also to Audi for sticking to normal aspiration when everyone else is flinging themselves headlong down the turbocharging route. Tightening emissions rules and the desire for more socially acceptable levels of fuel consumption have made this unavoidable, but Audi has managed to persist with a free-breathing engine in its craziest supercar. 'The V10 engine is the most powerful engine Audi has ever built. It is characterized by its linear response and a wide range of available power,' said Schala with possibly unintended understatement. 'The V10 is a very accessible motor – at all speeds you have immediate control of the power delivery.' No kidding.

The Audi's seven-speed auto is as seductive as it is scientific. It's harnessed to an all-wheel-drive system that uses an electronically actuated multi-plate clutch to channel all 602bhp to the rear wheels when you're on a dry road, elevating the entertainment experience to 8K IMAX levels of intimacy and interactivity. When you don't fancy your chances against Mother Nature, the R8 brings the front axle into play, offering face-bending levels of grip even in a monsoon.

Keeping the R8 under control is a task made much easier thanks to a mostly aluminium chassis, although there's carbon fibre in the transmission tunnel and rear firewall. The latest R8 is 40 per cent stiffer while being up to 50kg (110lb) lighter than its predecessor, and also shares half of its componentry with its endurance racing iteration. The road and GT3 race versions were codeveloped, which says much for the synergies described by Dr Ullrich.

The R8's powertrain really is a gem, each flick of the gearshift paddles dropping you into a never-ending vat of power and torque. If you can find the right road, or better still racetrack, the car's playfulness at low speed is matched only by its sublime balance as the speedo goes deep into three figures, and its aerodynamic cleverness manifests itself without you even noticing. It has downforce. A nod, too, to the R8's carbon ceramic brakes and unbelievable laser LED headlights; as much as I enjoy nudging a car up to the fabled 'ragged edge', I also like arriving home again in one piece. In terms of ease of use, the R8 is as user-friendly as it is fast.

It's also fun at zero mph. That's the speed I recommend until such time as you've fully mastered the 'virtual cockpit', which uses Nvidia processing firepower to perform 8.5 billion calculations per second. This gives the driver a satnav display of supernatural clarity and the ability to cycle through various media and entertainment modes, including a blistering audio system, although it has its work cut out challenging the sonic fireworks generated by that 10-cylinder engine.

BMW 7 Series
The return of the magnificent 7

BMW's 7 Series was so state-of-the-art it was almost like having your own digital chauffeur. The only thing left? Reinvent the wheel...

Back in 2002, archaeologists dredged up what is now thought to be the earliest recovered example of the wheel from the Ljubljana Marshes in Slovenia. They reckon it's up to 5,300 years old, which makes it a much younger innovation than you'd think. The wheel itself might well be older, but making it function properly required something more advanced: an axle. And that didn't happen until the Bronze Age. On the 24-hour clock of human evolution, that puts it at about two-and-half minutes before midnight.

Even so, it must frustrate the hell out of the German car industry that they can't reinvent the four round bits on the corners of their cars. The wheel is irritatingly unimprovable. Lord knows, they've tried to reimagine everything else, born of a conviction and confidence that's marrow-deep. The new BMW 7 Series epitomizes this titanic Teutonic self-belief. Only the kitchen sink is missing.

Of course, the big luxury limo has long been a mobile manifesto for technological superiority. Like its main rivals, Audi and Mercedes, BMW uses its plutocratic range-topper to showcase the next wave of tech, most of which will cascade down into the more proletarian end of the line later on. Crowd-pleasing stuff such as a semi-autonomous mode, self-parking, gesture control and a mini iPad-style key are all here. There is also a concierge service, and the 7 Series boasts such a profound degree of connectivity that it – and its ilk – risk dragging the automobile into our era-defining privacy debate. (Indeed, BMW has a fortified building stuffed with humming servers somewhere in Munich. I asked to visit it, and was firmly rebuffed, but I like to think the guy who runs it looks a bit like Christoph Waltz.)

In this context, and given that the person the 7 Series is aimed at is likely to remain a stranger to the front seat, it seems perverse to actually drive the thing. So that is exactly what I did. This is a process akin to being given the keys to a nuclear reactor without reading the instruction manual first.

There's that Display Key, for a start. The upside is that it has a trick swipe display showing the car's security status and can programme the climate control and even remote-park the car ('RCP' is an option). This tech has been around for a while now, but the BMW breakthrough is that the car's sensors and cameras are now clever enough to dispense with the driver. The downside is that, although as beautifully designed as anything by Jonathan Ive or Marc Newson, the key feels eminently losable (and costs £230 ($339) for a replacement).

ENGINE
2,993cc turbo diesel, 265bhp

PERFORMANCE
0–62mph in 6.1 secs; top speed 155mph (limited)

YEAR OF RELEASE
2016

PRICE ON RELEASE
£64,530 (not available in US)

Driving, then. Western masters of the universe might not bother, but in China – where a 7 Series owner's estimated average age is 28 – the chauffeur gets the weekend off and clients drive themselves. Although BMW has lately tweaked its ultimate driving machine mantra to include efficiency, the dynamism of its cars is a major USP. To which end, the new 7 Series features a 'carbon core', so that it incorporates carbon fibre in strategic areas of its body, including the sills, roof and central tunnel. Elsewhere you will find aluminium, magnesium and high-strength steel. It is all about shaving off weight, and when you factor in the new car's extra equipment, it's around 200kg (441lb) lighter.

And you can tell. The 730d – the range's big player – hits 62mph in just over six seconds, sits silently and effortlessly at 120mph on the Autobahn and can still return a claimed average of 60.1mpg and just 124g/km of CO_2. Even if you don't care, these are impressive figures for a car of this size and stature.

It's a real hustler, too. The chassis is fashionably configurable: 'Eco Pro' throttles back on the fun in pursuit of maximum saintliness; 'Sport' cedes control to the driver. But there's also an adaptive mode called 'Executive Drive Pro', which analyses your driving style and the satnav data to alter the powertrain and chassis accordingly. The car's sensors can read the road ahead, drawing the whole experience into a virtuous circle. Turn into a fast, tightening corner and the 7 Series holds its line and dearly wants to commit to the apex rather than wallowing about all over.

That's one option. The other is that you ignore all that silly stuff and enjoy the ride. The seats are fantastic, the headrests marshmallow soft, and eight different massage functions are available in the rear, along with an integrated 'Touch Command' tablet. There's also 4G, super-fast mobile broadband and ear-popping 16-speaker audio from Bowers & Wilkins, the level of which you can adjust using the thrillingly pointless gesture control (by miming a little circle in front of the central screen).

But what do I know? When my nine-year-old son sat in it, he uttered four words: 'This is the future.' And he's not wrong.

Mercedes-AMG GT
Winning the super bowl

In our first glimpse of the Mercedes-AMG GT, GQ leaned on the gas and took the car full camber on Europe's most vertigo-inducing Autodrome.

ENGINE
3,982cc V8, 462bhp
PERFORMANCE
0–62mph in 4.1 secs;
top speed 189mph
YEAR OF RELEASE
2014
PRICE ON RELEASE
£115,000 ($111,200)

'When you enter this building, you wind your watch forward five years,' observes Mercedes Chief Design Officer Gorden Wagener as he leads us along one of the 'fingers' of the company's HQ on the outskirts of Stuttgart, designed by Renzo Piano. It could just as easily be the hub of a biotech or computer company, such is the carefully engineered air of high achievement. Each area is arranged along a different slender concrete and steel digit, and access to the design division is so strictly monitored that *GQ* will later be escorted personally to the facilities during a 'comfort break'. Tinker, tailor, soldier, automotive journalist.

Today's revelation is the new AMG GT. It's the successor to the gull-winged SLS supercar, which was the first product wholly conceived by Mercedes' unstoppable performance division. Modishly, the new car is smaller, fleeter of foot and more environmentally acceptable, even as it squeezes 462bhp from its all-new 4.0-litre twin-turbo V8. Know-how derived from the –currently all-conquering – Mercedes-AMG Formula One operation has bequeathed the GT with an alloy cylinder head infused with zirconium, while the cylinders themselves are polished so rigorously they have a mirrored finish. An additional process called 'spectacle honing' even stops potential cylinder warping after final assembly.

You can't see that stuff, unless you keep an endoscopic camera in the glove box. But the stuff you can see is easier to understand and appreciate: the GT is a looker and no mistake. It's also the product of a constantly evolving narrative, one that Wagener sums up in two words: sensual purity.

'Mercedes is moving from being a traditional luxury company to a modern one,' he says. 'The concept of luxury changes over time. Right now, true luxury is a reduction; a focus on the things that truly matter. Western tastes have gone global, and simplicity is also an expression of modernity. That said, technology will change things more in the next 15 years than it's managed in the past 50.'

The GT is the perfect manifestation of this tension. On the one hand, Wagener's team now includes a small army dedicated purely to the headlights. It's all about LEDs and lasers these days, which in turn totally transform the aesthetics of a car's face. ('It's a good enabler for change,' says the boss.) Look closely enough, and the apparently simple act of illuminating the path ahead has become a highly complex affair. On the other hand, Mercedes' recent love affair with fussy body detailing is at an end. 'This is first-principles stuff,' Wagener says. 'Get the basics right and you can begin to reduce. The line that is not there is the highest precision for us.'

For all its painstakingly reduced complexity, there's something wonderfully old-fashioned about the way the AMG GT sits on the road. Retro is over, of course, but there are evocative images of the new car alongside Fifties Silver Arrows classics, the original 300 SL and SLR, on the design studio walls.

With good reason. The proportions are similar: turbine grille, long nose and broad, rounded shoulders. The GT looks very German, but there's a welcome infusion of Anglocentricity from some angles, too. With its front mid-engine and rear-transaxle-gearbox layout, there's also a distinct gap between the front wheel arch and the door. Get it wrong, and the whole thing becomes a pastiche. Get it right, and it looks like this. 'That,' smiles Wagener, 'we call the "prestige measurement". For me, though, the rear is the nicest part. You have to decide where to put the "real estate" and we put three feet of it into the car's shoulder. The more sporty the car, the bigger the shoulder.'

There's much to love inside, too, especially if aviation is your thing. There are six air vents, with four taking centre stage ahead of the multimedia screen, and their design mimics the look of a jet engine. The main instruments sit in a classic recessed binnacle. But the cabin is dominated by a huge centre console, whose shape references the NACA duct, the standard cooling inlet design used throughout the aeronautical and motorsport world. There are four buttons ranged on either side, a conscious reference to the GT's V8 configuration.

Mercedes has been very focused on interior quality recently, and the GT is, unsurprisingly, off the scale. There's a whole book to be written on how these guys configure their cabins and navigate regional idiosyncrasies – the Japanese don't like the smell of leather; there are 20,000 seat variations on the E-class saloon; you can order a real pinstripe inlay on the dash and door trim – but the GT manages to be ruthlessly driver-focused and also democratic. It's so well executed and all-enveloping that the passenger gets to have almost as much fun as the driver.

As Wagener himself adds, it's also potent enough to work as a piece of art. But what a waste that would be. This is for driving, and the countdown has begun.

Gumpert Apollo Sport
The riot act

Packing a powerful (224mph) punch, Gumpert's ultra-aerodynamic Apollo Sport rewrote the rules of the road.

You often read or hear something fun being described as a 'riot'. Now, I like The Clash as much as the next sentient music fan, and the word 'riot' has a certain onomatopoeic appeal. But as anyone who has watched an angry mob lose their minds in the heat of the moment would agree, a riot is as much fun as a brick in the head. Violence is never pretty.

Which brings me to the Gumpert Apollo Sport. It's not pretty and it's extremely violent. This car will actively try to beat you up. Tap in to its straight-line acceleration and you will end up bruised. Throttle-off slightly in between each brutally fast gear change (less than 50 milliseconds!), and a noise erupts from somewhere in the belly of the beast that sounds as friendly as a medieval battlefield. The Gumpert, then, is a riot. A mobile warzone. It is not of this earth.

Actually, it's screwed together in a converted sewing mill in Altenberg, a small town 30 miles south of Leipzig in eastern Germany. This is another thing that marks it out as a little unusual: 30 years since the Berlin Wall came down, you'll still see the relics of that age trundling around – profoundly unlovely Wartburgs, Trabants and Barkas vans – into the midst of which the mid-engined, 750bhp Gumpert has arrived with all the subtlety of Nicki Minaj joining a church choir. I've driven most things, and I can honestly say that the Apollo is as extreme as anything with four wheels and an engine is ever likely to get.

Like many of these ultra-rare-groove supercars, it only exists because of a man with a 'vision'. Former Audi motorsport boss Roland Gumpert figured that even the wildest Porsches and Ferraris weren't really wild enough, and that if he could deliver a genuinely race-bred experience, then (very rich) people would come. (Not so much a field of dreams as a converted sewing mill, but anyway...)

And, to some extent, they have: Gumpert has made close to 60 cars since the business started in 2005, and the car I'm driving today – the latest, most powerful S version – will head to Hong Kong when I'm finished with it. It also costs a thumping £500,000 ($965,000).

To be blunt, this is a Le Mans-style endurance-racing car, made legal. Its chassis is a race-car-style web of lightweight, high-strength chrome-

ENGINE
4.2-litre twinturbo V8, 750bhp

PERFORMANCE
0–62mph in 2.9 secs; top speed 224mph

YEAR OF RELEASE
2005

PRICE ON RELEASE
From £468,000 ($904,000)

molybdenum steel tubes with a carbon-fibre tub moulded into it. It's so aerodynamically extreme that it generates enough downforce for it to be driven upside down on the roof of a tunnel, theoretically at least. An odd boast, perhaps, but also one that can only be made by modern Formula One cars, and you don't see them on the high street very often.

Less odd are the performance claims: 0–62mph in 2.9 seconds; 0–124mph in 8.8 seconds; top speed of 224mph. This is what 750bhp charged with moving just 1,250kg (1.38 tonnes) can do, although it's definitely at the far end of an already seriously elongated envelope.

Luckily, Gumpert has access to an old Soviet air base on which to verify these outlandish claims. I didn't need a stopwatch to confirm that the Apollo is a new magnitude of fast: unhappy internal organs were proof enough, plus the fact that, even on a runway, minus all the usual reference points (trees, hedges, other traffic), this thing felt cosmically quick. It's best to drive it like a racing car, too, which is to say respectfully, handling it like you'd handle, say, nitroglycerine.

The Gumpert is designed to grip in a way that most cars simply aren't, has vast Michelin Pilot Super Sport tyres, and furiously turns the air that passes over it into downforce. Interrupt any part of that process and things could get very nasty, very quickly. It's a scary car, all right, and one in which intimations of pilot mortality are never far away. Paradoxically, I haven't felt so alive driving a car in ages.

Chapter 3
Best of British

For an island nation that built its reputation on naval supremacy, we haven't done too badly in the car stakes over the years. Of course, we've hit a few speed bumps along the way (you won't find much of the British Leyland canon here), but ultimately we have produced world-beating racing cars, sector-defining brands, and staked a claim to creating the most famous marques in automotive history. In other words, we feel we should be rightly proud of Jaguar, Bentley and Rolls-Royce. But there is more to this sceptred isle than big cats, winged Bs and the Spirit of Ecstasy. There is also the quintessential craftsmanship of Bristol, the iconic embodiment of legendary superspy James Bond that is Aston Martin and, most recently, the inexorable rise of Formula One racing legend turned sports car manufacturer McLaren. So when we say Best of British, we think we might be onto something...

Aston Martin Vanquish
Ride of the century

To celebrate Aston Martin's 100th birthday in 2013, GQ *took on the indefatigable grit of a limited-edition Vanquish.*

Although Aston Martin recently celebrated hitting the big 1-0-0, *GQ* has been tracking the great marque's adventure especially closely for the past few years. Back in 2003, *GQ* was the first in the world to drive the DB9, the svelte opening salvo in a brand offensive that went on to encompass a rousing return to Le Mans, the rehousing and rehabilitation of a certain cinematic spy, a wave of effortlessly beautiful new cars and a successful Chinese invasion, all while riding the vicissitudes of an economic downturn of unusual duration.

Aston Martin has fallen foul of a few of those in the past, with various well-meaning patrons and entrepreneurs – and even schoolboy pocket-money donations – desperately fuelling the dream during the company's previous 90 years. Returning to the Aston HQ in 2013 – a building best described as a modernist castle, and only partially finished last time we were here – with the latest Centenary Edition Vanquish and the immortal DB5 for company, is a reminder that while things have gone full circle, this particular circle isn't a circle at all so much as a Möbius strip.

Running a company like Aston Martin against big, profitable and acutely tech-savvy players like Bentley, Ferrari and Porsche is not for the faint-hearted or the tightfisted. Six months ago Aston had to recapitalize, and raised £150 million ($232 million) from Italian private-equity firm Investindustrial in return for a 37.5 per cent stake. That sort of money will barely touch the sides but, crucially, it reinforces Aston's attractiveness and credibility to the potential technology partners and suppliers it urgently needs to sway. Why? Because the same basic components matrix has underpinned virtually every Aston since 2003, and the engine and transmission are no longer state-of-the-very-fast-moving-art. This is the stuff that requires huge investment.

Not that the Vanquish lacks credibility per se. The latest and most powerful Aston GT so far, the Vanquish contains 75 per cent new parts and its bonded-aluminium tub now features plenty of carbon fibre (as do the body panels). It's 25 per cent stiffer than the DBS it replaces, and 85 per cent of the Vanquish's mass sits within the wheelbase. The front chassis structure is 13 per cent lighter than the DBS's, and the six-litre V12 sits 19mm (^{3}/$_4$in) lower in the car and now pumps out 565bhp. The suspension uses double wishbones all round, with continuously variable active damping (ADS), the parameters of which are governed by whether you're in normal, sport or track mode, controlled by a red button on the steering wheel. Unsurprisingly, it's also extremely fast.

ENGINE
6.0-litre V12, 565bhp
PERFORMANCE
0–62mph in 4.1 secs;
top speed 183mph
YEAR OF RELEASE
2012 (second generation)
PRICE ON RELEASE
£200,000 (approx.)
($279,995)

The Centenary Edition adds even greater exclusivity – only 100 will be made – and the modifications are subtle to the point of classy invisibility: the wing badges are in sterling silver and enamel, the paintwork has a graduated finish that takes 68 hours to complete, the black leather inside was previously the preserve of the £1m One-77 supercar, and customers even receive a personalized presentation box containing a pair of glass keys, solid-silver cufflinks and Bang & Olufsen headphones. There's also a matching silver polishing cloth to maintain that sweeping, swooping bodywork (though Vanquish owners may have a minion on the payroll to take care of that part of the deal). It's hugely seductive and exemplifies an ownership experience none of Aston's rivals can match.

Aston's former CEO, Dr Ulrich Bez, famously summed up the appeal of the brand: 'An Aston Martin is one of the few cars you could identify even if you took the badges off. It will always have the grill, the proportions, the same dynamic body language, and it is refined,' he explains. 'There are lots of supercars you would struggle to recognize if you painted them red, parked them side by side, and removed their badges. As long as we make sports cars, they will look like Aston Martins. 'We have produced 50,000 cars since 2000, which compares favourably to the 65,000 we have made overall in the company's 100-year history,' he adds with a wry flourish.

No doubt about that. The new Vanquish is a more accessible, civilized and less aggressive proposition than its forebear. It soaks up big crests and laughs off nasty compressions in the road. Dr Bez talks about 'balance', and the Vanquish has it. The cabin has a unique atmosphere, and the centre console buttons deliver a 'haptic' buzz when you touch them – a memorable innovation. But is it enough to profitably propel Aston Martin deep into the 21st century?

'Look, in principle this is a fair question. A small company like ours doesn't have the same resources as, say, Porsche,' Dr Bez says, frustration now simmering on a low heat. 'But a more respectful [question] would involve appreciating what we do with the resources we have. Next, what do we do differently to the big players? We are not necessarily the first to market with some technologies because that costs a lot of money. But in my opinion it's not important to be the first in the luxury sector, it's important to be the best.'

It's an approach that might just see them right for the next 100 years.

Rolls-Royce Wraith
Wraith of the titans

Elegant, intelligent and the most potent Rolls-Royce ever, the Wraith was the new driving force in luxury engineering.

ENGINE
6.6-litre twin-turbo V12, 624bhp

PERFORMANCE
0–62mph in 4.6 secs; top speed 155mph (limited)

YEAR OF RELEASE
2013

PRICE ON RELEASE
£215,000 ($288,600)

The Rolls-Royce Wraith is a motorcar powered by a paradox. That may sound like something from an episode of *Star Trek*, but it's the conundrum that lies at the heart of this phenomenal...device. (Is it really a car? I'm not sure.)

It goes like this. The Wraith is a 'masterpiece of elegant simplicity' that also happens to be such an obsidian presence on the road that you need planning permission to park it. With a 624bhp, 6.6-litre twin-turbo V12, it's also the most powerful car in the company's history. Yet it's been engineered to waft not sprint, because an overt demonstration of its potential is frankly unseemly. And despite being one of the world's great status symbols, Rolls-Royce in general somehow exempts itself from fashionable class-war unpleasantness. (Maybe the fact that both Lenin and working-class hero John Lennon owned Rolls-Royces has something to do with it.)

A lot of nonsense is talked about what luxury means in the modern era. Well, trust me, the Wraith is the real deal. You would never do anything as proletarian as book a test drive in one of these, so much as have your people talk to its people, then ready the jet for an appointment. Walking towards it in the pit lane of Goodwood racing circuit – the Rolls-Royce assembly plant is only a few miles away – the Wraith positively heaves with presence, as imposing as a stately home but just as wilfully odd in many ways as the British aristocracy.

For a start, it's a fastback rather than a coupé, an unusual format that expertly evokes the louche automotive excesses of the Twenties and early Thirties, and imposes a timely Gatsby-esque narrative on a car that F Scott Fitzgerald's literary cipher would surely have adored. The famous Rolls pantheon grille is subtly recessed, the bonnet is even longer than before, it's wider at the back, the windscreen is raked, and even the famous Spirit of Ecstasy mascot is less recondite and more receptive looking.

True, these refinements are subtle to the point of invisibility, but they add up to a whole that delivers on that thoroughly debased, oft-evoked notion: uniqueness. It also has a tangibly saturnine quality, positioning this particular Rolls more in an after-hours Miami milieu than the midday Sussex vibe we're currently experiencing, but you can't have everything.

Of course, a car like the Wraith is meant to be an event. Should you glimpse one, you're supposed to post as much on Instagram at your earliest convenience. This is one of those vehicles designed to throw off a dividend of pleasure akin to a work of art, which is oddly democratic for a £200,000+ ($280,000+) car. The only problem is that the Wraith's occupants will always be having a better time than you. As lofty as an SUV, access to the car's cabin is via giant rear-hinged 'coach doors'.

There are nautical and aeronautical touches aplenty inside, as well as the option of Canadel-wood panelling, while 1,340 individual fibre optics can be woven into the headlining for a starlight effect. As in so many areas of the Wraith, its creators manage to dazzle where so many disappoint. This sportier iteration of the Rolls ideal gets a chunkier steering wheel, but the rest of the cabin is pretty much the same gloriously monolithic slab of Art Deco as before. A pair of weighted rotary sliders even control the air conditioning, rendering one of the dullest jobs in a car with an appreciable tactility. Rolls talks up its voice-activation software, but my Irish accent repeatedly defeated it. Apparently, it's better with Mandarin.

After all that theatre, the Wraith runs the outside risk of being an anti-climactic driving machine. But it's not. Nothing else out there moves with the same blend of patrician poise and outright dynamism. Despite its weight and girth, it's genuinely fast, and it grips and handles superbly, although swift sorties down country roads really ought to be telegraphed in advance by a valet.

Which brings me on to the Wraith's undoubted party piece: its Satellite Aided Transmission (SAT). There's no paradoxical steampunk sci-fi at work here: by combining the navigation system and GPS data, the Wraith scans the road ahead and figures out which of the eight gears it should select based on current location and driver behaviour. Who knew that Big Brother would arrive in such an elegantly tailored form?

Jaguar F-Type V6 S
Cool for cats

Despite some legendary and iconic competition, Jaguar's F-Type could hold its own against any of the marque's classics.

ENGINE
2,995cc supercharged V6, 375bhp

PERFORMANCE
0–62mph in 4.8 secs; top speed 171mph

YEAR OF RELEASE
2013

PRICE ON RELEASE
£67,520 ($81,000)

Daniel Day-Lewis's thespian intensity is well known to the film-going public. It's part of an armoury of skills that has won him three Best Actor Oscars, and he's the only person in movie history to have managed it. But right now, the furrowed concentration on his face is the real thing, and he doesn't look especially happy. 'I used to cycle and run when I was at school, and I could never figure out the split times then, either,' he says darkly. 'All I could do was subtract. I played a lot of darts during my misspent youth, you see...'

It's the day before the start of the Mille Miglia, Italy's legendary road race. From Brescia to Rome and then back north again via Siena, Florence and Modena, the original event ran from 1927–57, an implausibly Italian blend of glamour, lithe machinery and automotive derring-do. Stirling Moss, famously, set a never-beaten record in 1955, when he drove his Mercedes 300 SLR to victory on the 1,000 miles in a still barely believable ten hours, seven minutes and 48 seconds.

Two years later, the fame turned to notoriety when Ferrari driver Alfonso de Portago crashed out, killing himself, his co-driver and nine spectators. And that was that, for a while, anyway. The resurrected Mille Miglia has been run – at a slightly more genteel pace – since 1977, with 375 cars challenging for honours. Only cars made between 1927 and 1957 are eligible, and the line-up is as varied as it is valuable.

Alfa Romeo, BMW, Ferrari, Porsche and Mercedes all leverage the Mille Miglia to bathe their current line-up in the fuzzy afterglow generated by their old-timers, although anyone who's ever driven the Passo della Futa at speed will tell you that the rush you get is more than purely Proustian. This is properly hard-core.

It's a competition, with timed stages and tricky trials that require deft driving and astute navigation. This is the bit Daniel Day-Lewis and his co-driver the movie mogul Jim Gianopulos, along with fellow competitors David Gandy, Yasmin Le Bon and Sir Chris Hoy, are grappling with. *GQ* is tasked with shadowing Day-Lewis and Gianopulos's 1950 Jaguar XK120 in something that, while wildly ineligible, is every bit as elegant: the brand new F-Type.

If it feels a little fraudulent, it's also a relief as we leave Brescia, roads still glinting from relentless rainfall. Right now, I quite fancy the idea of decent brakes and roadholding. Jaguar, for so long haunted by its heritage and the E-Type in particular, is happy to evoke the granddaddy of British sports cars with its new baby. The F-Type bristles with a tightly packed menace, like a flyweight pugilist, but the promise of violence is offset by some deft design details. Oddly enough, its rear end has an Italianate sensuousness, all hips, slender lights and minimal decoration. Modern tech sits cheek by jowl alongside old-school switchgear and materials without feeling contrived. There's character and maybe even soul, commodities the otherwise generally superior German competition can't quite muster.

Ours is the V6 S model, so it's packing a 3.0-litre supercharged V6 that produces 375bhp (there's a lesser V6 and a rocket-ship 488bhp V8). This gives us a stratospheric advantage over the Day-Lewis/Gianopulos XK120, but those guys aren't hanging about. Day-Lewis is an accomplished biker, Gianopulos a serial classic-car owner and Mille Miglia veteran, and each appreciates how to wring the best from a 63-year-old motorcar (insert jokes about left-foot braking here...).

Several other things stand out: first, this car is knocking on the door of supercar fast, hammering to 60mph in under five seconds and on to 171mph before the carabinieri have time to blink under their Wayfarers. Second, its exhaust crackles and pops with all the subtlety of machine-gun fire ricocheting off a metal bin lid. It's hopelessly extrovert behaviour, and particularly enjoyable with the roof lowered. Finally, the F-Type loves to go sideways, even with the traction control on and especially on a damp road, so be warned. It needs a firm hand, which is just as it should be. This is a car that has been designed and engineered by people who clearly know how to have a good time, and you will too, provided you're up for it. It's a vinyl record in a world of digital downloads; a full-fat sports car. And, even in the midst of the titans contesting the Mille Miglia, a proper Jaguar.

McLaren 720S
The Mac is back

For their 2017 Maranello-beater, Woking's wunderkinds tore up the rulebook. GQ *took the McLaren 720S from town to track and found a dizzying six-figure speedster to rival the £1 million monsters.*

McLaren has parked its new tank on Ferrari's lawn. The 720S is unusually aerodynamic for a tank, considerably lighter and much, much faster, but as Rome rubs the sleep out of its eyes, our first taste of this new British supercar will take us close to Caracalla, scene of Ferrari's first racing victory, just over 70 years ago. A mischievous coincidence.

The Italian legends have done more than most in the intervening decades to locate the sweet spot between artisanship and engineering. The company was presided over by a potentate, Enzo Ferrari, whose towering personality and guile proved as good at crafting a narrative as it was at creating cars. This was a man who wore sunglasses indoors on even the darkest day to prevent his eyes from betraying his mood.

McLaren Automotive is barely into its second decade, so it can't compete on age, even if its racing division dates back to 1963 and famously employed a certain Ayrton Senna in his imperial phase. But something special's going on, because the 720S is one of the most singularly impressive motorcars of all time. In replacing the 650S, Woking has embarked on its very own moonshot, with otherworldly results.

McLaren says 91 per cent of the 720S is new, and the enlarged 4.0-litre V8 engine features 41 per cent new content: turbos, intercoolers, cylinder heads, crankshaft, pistons and exhaust. This equates to a power output of 710bhp, 568lb ft of torque, 0–62mph in 2.9 seconds and 0–124mph in 7.8, and the ability to brake from that same speed in just 4.6 seconds and 117m (128 yards). You want a weapons analogy? This is more of an intercontinental ballistic missile than a tank.

It was actually Lamborghini, not Ferrari, that set the template for the mid-engined supercar more than 50 years ago with the incomparable Miura. Its body had the curvaceous grace of a *Dolce Vita*-era Cinecittà movie star, but it was an intimidating, often truculent driving experience.

In 2017, McLaren has delivered a car that is as easy to pilot around Italy's chaotic capital as a Fiat Panda and possibly even easier to see out of. The 720S upends the diktat that says cars like this should punish the driver until they're in full flight: its ride is plush and it's quiet when you want it to be. But while the McLaren's operating window is vastly larger than anyone would have dared

ENGINE
4.0-litre V8, 710bhp
PERFORMANCE
0–62mph in 2.9 secs;
top speed 211.9mph
YEAR OF RELEASE
2017
PRICE ON RELEASE
£208,600 ($297,100)

dream 50 years ago, it still generates maximum theatre in terms of its visuals, even if its complexity and the need for unprecedented aerodynamic efficiency stops it from being naturally beautiful.

'Design is where you bring all the elements together,' the 720S' principal architect, Rob Melville, explains. 'Styling is just one aspect of it. We want to create breathtaking products that tell you the visual story of their function and we're guided by four things. Nature, and the idea of "functional jewellery". We want to be true with the materials we use – it has to be authentic. The proportions need to be perfect. And we are always brave. The dihedral doors were the biggest challenge. We did feel the pain getting those right. You don't open them so much as begin unpeeling the car.'

That process turns out to be deeply satisfying. The 720S somehow combines the ergonomic efficiency of a racing car with the technical luxury of a modern GT. The principal readouts are housed directly ahead, as you'd expect, but the 'folding display' is genuinely innovative, the idea being that you can focus on the most important information if you're on a track. This is a car with multiple moods, a consciously engineered bipolarity that's overseen by a series of drive mode controls that live in a vertical pod to the left of the wheel. The D, N and R buttons are in another pod that tapers flamboyantly towards the bottom. There's also a breathtaking 1,280-watt audio system, whose speakers are seamlessly blended into the ebb and flow of the interior. It feels more like wiring yourself into an organism than jumping into a car.

Driving anything around Rome is a risky enterprise at the best of times, but the 720S is easy. Buzzing hordes of hyperactive Vespas fail to disappear into a blind spot, because there aren't any. Tyre noise and mechanical thrum are negligible at regular cruising speeds. In fact, in terms of ease of use, you could almost be in an airport rental.

Turn up the heat, though, and the McLaren does what anything that can warp to 60mph in less than three seconds does: compress time. Fast hatchbacks can do that age-old increment in under five seconds, which wins a certain amount of bragging rights. A select few cars can do it in less than four. But beating three seconds is when forward motion happens faster than your brain can really process it, and the McLaren keeps on keeping on, reeling in the horizon with a relentlessness that borders on the surreal.

Shift times on the seven-speed dual-shift box are 45 per cent faster than even the manic limited series 675 LT delivered, and its performance is on a par with the £1 million ($1.15 million) P1 hypercar. You can sense the chassis electronics doing their thing, but they're so expertly calibrated that any intervention is almost imperceptible. Even then, you'll have to be pushing very hard indeed. The 720S' limits aren't merely sky-high, they're stratospheric.

McLaren let *GQ* loose on a brilliant circuit called Vallelunga, an hour's drive north of Rome – the scene of old-school derring-do by many of Italy's most celebrated post-war racing heroes. There are plenty of opportunities here to make a fool of yourself, but the 720S lets you choose between fast, very fast and 'are we really going that fast?'. According to McLaren, the new variable drift control software 'delivers additional enjoyment in sport and track modes, with fingertip control of electronic stability control intensity' and if that sort of showboating is your thing, just turn it all off and revel in the car's awesome chassis. McLaren uses a similar nine-stage traction control system on its GT race cars, and the company's raconteur-ish chief test driver reckons it helps optimize setup for whichever track you regularly visit. The 720S' integrated telemetry software is another push in that direction but, frankly, I think you'd be barmy to go anywhere near a circuit in your £208,600 ($297,100) McLaren.

And that's at the cheaper end of the spectrum: start working your way through the options list and things get very expensive very quickly. Much of the 720S is made of carbon fibre, but even so a three-part carbon exterior upgrade package is an additional £18,000 ($22,230). Inside, you'll need another £3,180 ($3,860) for carbon-fibre seat backs. Hell, even the parking sensors are £1,000 ($3,010) (no carbon there, either). *GQ*'s test car actually featured £74,000 ($91,000) of extras.

On the other hand, the 720S is the best McLaren since 1993's unicorn-rare F1 and you won't find one of those for less than about £8 million ($9.85 million) nowadays. Perversely, then, this new car isn't just brilliant, it's also a bargain.

Aston Martin Vantage
Flying colours

Aston Martin had a lot riding on its new Vantage. Aggressive, sophisticated and cloaked in the boldest shades on the road, it was a brave evolution of the brand's bestselling car. Think things are always greener on the other side? Not from this driving seat...

ENGINE
4.0-litre twin-turbo V8, 503bhp
PERFORMANCE
0–62mph in 3.7 secs; top speed 195mph
YEAR OF RELEASE
2017
PRICE ON RELEASE
£115,000 ($149,995)

Incredibly, plenty of people don't know anything about cars and care even less. When pressed, however, they'll offer some vacuous observation about the colour. As if whatever hue a car is painted actually defines it. Then you see a car like Aston Martin's Vantage, photographed exclusively for *GQ* and presented here in Lime Essence. And this actually matters, because this is Aston Martin getting very punchy with the replacement for the bestselling car in its history, the one that needs to hit pay dirt straight out of the box.

'It is deliberate,' says Aston's chief designer Miles Nurnberger. 'We came up with a colour for the previous Vantage race car called Stirling Green. It was for inserts, then we thought, "Let's do the whole thing." We're seeing interest in a wider spread of colours in our global markets. The new Vantage on display in our Gaydon HQ is bright red. We're pushing things forward.'

Something similar is going on at Ferrari, whose cars also transcend mere transport to become art. But no piece of art I'm aware of has to stick to the ground at 200mph or protect its owners if all goes wrong. In other words, Aston Martin, like Ferrari, has to perform an aesthetic conjuring trick that reconciles the demands of physics, as well as legislation governing pedestrian safety, with the need for beauty. What good is an ugly Aston Martin?

Now have another look at the nose on the new Vantage, and the way the sheet metal plunges downward. There are contours and radii on the front wings and bonnet that have to trigger the right responses, while doing a functional job. Aston is good at curves, but a sports car also needs tension, volume and stance to stop the whole thing from collapsing. That can lead to a profusion of lines, and a car that looks too busy is a car that isn't working. Right now, reductionism is very fashionable in car design.

The Vantage challenges some norms; there's a lot of aero – particularly on the rear end – and Nurnberger's team has gone minimal with the head-and tail-lights. It is a complicated car striving for simplicity, and that's the hardest trick of all.

'We know people criticize,' Nurnberger says candidly. 'but I'd be more upset if people said we hadn't moved on enough. Just a few years ago, Marek [Reichman, CCO] and I decided that we needed to reimagine what Aston Martin stands for. The new Vantage is sportier, more aggressive, and we've lost the veined metal grille. This'll upset some people, no doubt. Aston got very good recently at taking one strand of its design and really refining it. But there were many more strands in the past and we want to explore them all again.'

The DB11, the Vantage's big brother, is the GT car, the gentleman in coat-tails. The new car, Nurnberger says, is the hunter, a car with the scent of blood in its nostrils. 'There's an urgency built into it; we wanted it to look like its character. And it consciously moves the Aston story on. Our design was very progressive in the past. It will be again.'

The new Vantage is another car whose dash-to-axle ratio has been improved; it's only 10mm (³/₈in) longer than the old car, but the front wheels are 65mm (2¹/₂in) further forward, and the rears 20mm (³/₄in) further back, so it looks meaner and more sophisticated. Inside, the Vantage revels in its switchgear and is better packaged and more cosseting.

One of the most prominent buttons turns off the traction control. Chief chassis guru Matt Becker says the shorter platform gives it more honest responses, underlining its sportier nature. It's also the first Aston to get an electronic differential, so while its front end 'feels like it'll never give up', and benefits from the incisiveness of torque vectoring, the stability at its near-200mph top speed is just as resolute.

To be clear, whatever colour you go for, the Vantage should be the most accessibly driver-centric Aston Martin ever. Aston's deal with Mercedes yields one of the world's best engines in its 4.0-litre, twin-turbo V8, which makes 503bhp here. It's also destined to succeed the old car as one of the most successful customer racing cars in endurance motorsport history. Look out for the Lime Essence at Le Mans and beyond.

Bristol Fighter
Flight of fancy

Ultra-exclusive and unashamedly old-school, Bristol's prized Fighter left other supercars in its turbocharged wake. GQ joined the jet set and (finally) took one for a test drive.

ENGINE
8.0-litre V10, 525bhp
PERFORMANCE
0–62mph in 4 secs;
top speed 210mph
YEAR OF RELEASE
2008
PRICE ON RELEASE
£235,000 ($471,000)

Despite constant claims that the age of international austerity is still with us and that most economies are on the brink of yet another recession, from Holland Park to the Hamptons the planet's 'high-net-worth' individuals are still merrily disposing of their high net worth at every opportunity. Cars, art, property...it was ever thus. These are not Bristol people, however. Granted, at £235,000 ($471,000) apiece an almost comical degree of liquidity is required to get yourself behind the wheel of the Fighter. But the appeal of a car such as this lies somewhere north of discerning. Just don't call them 'eccentric'.

Bristol has been making cars since 1946, when the cessation of wartime hostilities saw its robust engineering skills diverted into the automotive sector. In the early Sixties, a former racing driver called Tony Crook took control. And as the company turned into the motoring equivalent of an obscure but cherished Savile Row tailor, Crook paid tramps to sit on rivals' motor show stands, and used unorthodox sales techniques. He was also Peter Sellers' 'manager of motoring affairs' so, aside from all the mischief, he must have been a man of infinite patience.

Rarely has Bristol made more than 150 cars per year. Under new ownership since 2001, the business has been built on keeping most of the 10,000 or so autos in existence alive. The Fighter was the company's first new car for about 35 years, launched with minimal fanfare in 2003, and each one took upwards of four months to complete. Clearly, this was a car for people who regard Astons, Bentleys and Ferraris as riffraff. It took me five years to arrange a test drive.

Powered by a 525bhp Chrysler V10, the Fighter moves with a strangely lazy energy, but ingenious aerodynamics help it achieve an alleged top speed of 210mph. A 1,036bhp twin-turbocharged version has a theoretical top speed of 270mph, but you'd have to be more than merely eccentric to verify that. It's surprisingly easy to drive for such a powerful thing, but both the engine and transmission are from the Dark Ages. You half expect the brakes to be operated by a lever on the outside of the car.

Then again, that's surely the point. Bristol's boss got angry with me when I suggested the company was wilfully stuck in the Stone Age. But with increasingly intrusive technology sucking the life out of the supercar, the Bristol Fighter is a gloriously old-school auto that wipes the floor with its rivals – principally because it hasn't really got any.

The GQ Bentley Arnage
Designer drive

The Bentley Arnage got the GQ treatment.

ENGINE
6.75-litre V8, 500bhp
PERFORMANCE
0–62mph in 5.9 secs;
top speed 168mph
YEAR OF RELEASE
2004
PRICE ON RELEASE
From £160,000 ($208,385)

Many invitations arrive at Britain's only quality men's monthly demanding to be worked over roughly with the old journalistic backhoe, 'It was a dirty job, but someone had to do it.' Most command our presence at a supermodel casting or require we visit a 'destination' hotel. If times are particularly hard, we are summoned to a vertical tasting of vintage champagnes. All grim stuff, to be sure, and each, in their own way, deserving of that oh-so-ironic opener.

But the mother of this pitiable strand of hard-laboured journalese came our way last autumn when *GQ* was invited to 'order' our very own Bentley Arnage. Each year, the venerable car company commissions a highly specified example of its pre-eminent four-door performance saloon to serve in its press fleet. It was this vehicle *GQ* was chosen to customize. It was a dirty job...oh, never mind.

Bentley has been producing legendary leviathans since 1921 and, since 2003, has built the world's fastest street-legal coupé in the shape of the Continental GT. Indeed, so successful has been the GT it's tempting to think of this svelte beauty as the only car with which Bentley busies itself. But this is far from the truth. GTs are purring off the production line at a rapid rate, thanks mainly to a plan devised by parent company VW, whereby cars are assembled in-house before being 'topped off' with VW's mighty twin-turbo, six-litre, 12-cylinder engine imported from Germany. Next to the GT line, however, work on Bentley's traditional four-door luxury performance saloon continues at a more sedate pace. Despite the competition from its £110,000 ($149,990) half-brother, with everything hand-built and/or hand-finished here, the £160,000 ($208,385) Arnage R is the essence of Bentley – a marriage of beauty and brawn in a one-of-a-kind package, thanks to the number of permutations available to the buyer.

Quite how many permutations became apparent when *GQ* settled in to the buyer's suite to play with the computer-imaging program Bentley has devised to bring the thousands of options alive. It's here that buyers peruse colour charts and leather samples, admire the marquetry-to-metalworking skills that go into a custom-built car and let their imaginations – and platinum cards – run wild.

From the comfort of this viewpoint, it's a small finger-stretch to specifying contrasting stitching on the upholstery, a humidor in the boot to house one's road-going Havanas, an armrest fridge to chill that cheeky half-bottle of Krug, and a DVD system with headrest-mounted screens. All of which we...er...did.

Going 'textbook' meant opting not only for the Arnage T model (the Black Label denotes an uprated 6.75-litre twin-turbo-charged V8 engine with a performance that six-times Le Mans winner and Bentley test driver Derek Bell once told *GQ*, is a 'bit of a handful') and ordering a gunmetal paint job, teamed with British racing green interior – a nod to Bentley's reputation as a luxury sporting marque without equal (four Le Mans wins, the last in 2003). Next, we upgraded to the sports package, which includes the milled-aluminium dash, side 'gills', 19in alloy rims and some subtly contrasting stitching to complement the exterior. Finally, Bentley suggested tailor-made headrests, radio cover and running boards to remind all those who voyage in her that this had been commissioned by *GQ*.

As the options added up, so did the bill. This had started at £160,000 ($208,385) for the 'basic' Arnage R model, but topped out at nearly £200,000 ($265,385). And that was without even setting foot in the Mulliner limousine department, where cars are bespoked to an even greater degree. Here, long wheel-based Arnages are fitted with every conceivable luxury, from passenger privacy screens to armour plating. Such is the nature of this work – the Queen's last limousine was manufactured here – that Bentley employs an in-house artist to render the imaginings of the typically obsessive Bentley Mulliner client. And yet, the popularity of the service has prompted Bentley to offer a limited production run of 25 cars over the next two years, starting at £270,000 ($350,00) each.

But *GQ*'s Bentley Arnage...well, we think it's priceless.

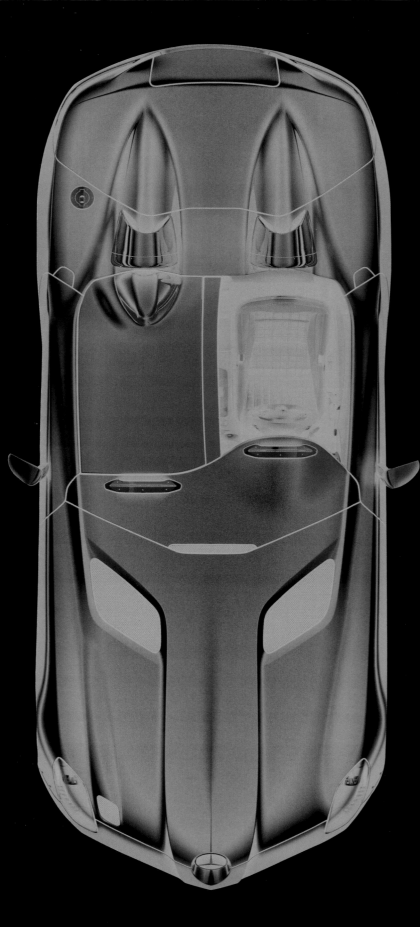

Chapter 4
Concept Cars

The purpose of a concept car is not necessarily to showcase what is coming soon, but to demonstrate the potential of possibility. It could be a revolutionary styling theory, an ambitious technological prediction, or even a statement of just how bonkers the designers can be when given a little latitude with their creations. Every manufacturer has flexed their modelling muscles over the years and, like the mystery of life and Forrest Gump's fabled box of chocolates, you never really know what you are going to get from each unveiling. And to be honest, sometimes *GQ* has been unable to resist showcasing the boldest and most innovative examples. From perhaps the most iconic concept car ever created (the Mercedes-Benz C111) through to Honda's exciting real-world attempt at producing the first hydrogen-powered car (the FCX), we've always been a sucker for the sensational...so much so that, with a little help (OK, make that a lot) from Citroën, we built our own. Not many magazines can say that.

GQ by Citroën
The GQ Citroën concept car

From drawing board to driving seat: how Britain's No. 1 men's magazine joined forces with 2010's definitive carmaker, and Savile Row, to produce the GQ by Citroën.

We've had made-to-measure suits, personalized aftershaves, handmade shoes and limited-edition accessories. We've given our name to racehorses, bars and houses. So it was only a matter of time before *GQ* took its penchant for the bespoke to its logical conclusion: its very own concept car. After careful consultation with French automotive design legends Citroën, months of development, creative brilliance and a smattering of Savile Row magic, here it is...

THE BRIEF – by Dylan Jones, *GQ* Editor

When Citroën proposed the idea, I was initially sceptical, because I wasn't quite sure what its aspirations were. But it sounded like an idea with potential, so we took the meeting. Lucky for us because it only took a matter of minutes for me to become totally excited by the prospect of designing a car for the company. In broad brushstrokes, I wanted something practical, something cool and something idiosyncratic, i.e., something surprising that didn't just look like a concept car. The *GQ* car needed to have the 'want' factor, but it also needed to look, feel and 'drive' like the sort of car no sane man could ignore.

A high bar, for sure, but then I figured if Citroën was offering to produce the car, the least we could do was give it a decent blueprint. And are we happy with the result? What do you think? We think it looks very, very special.

THE DESIGN – by Domagoj Dukec, Citroën Design Supervisor

I've always read *GQ* and it is a magazine that communicates my lifestyle, so I had some feelings about what we could create, but what we took from Dylan was an idea of the spirit of *GQ*, what it represents, and how that could be transcribed into a vehicle. The words that stuck in my mind were 'elegance', 'refinement' and, above all, 'tailored'.

For me, the car that has always represented the pinnacle of automotive excellence and refinement is the grand tourer (GT). It is not the all-out sports car; it is something gentlemanly. It has performance, and it is for travelling, not racing. With the *GQ* car, we wanted something close to a shooting brake, but one that would look as good driving to the theatre. Dylan mentioned a further two words that resonated with that vision: 'sexy' and 'practical'. It is the practical element that gives this car more character.

ENGINE
1,598cc 4-cylinder Hybrid4, 200bhp

PERFORMANCE
0–62mph in 4.5 secs; top speed 155mph

YEAR OF DESIGN
2010

The car we've created is unique. It is not a variant of an existing vehicle. It stands alone. We wanted to create something that, as with *GQ*, was aspirational, but also retains the classic automotive ideals.

To realize this, we took the basic GT concept and applied the classic two-box Citroën styling to create something refined but not ostentatious. When we were designing it, we didn't follow the traditional path of having many designers working on ideas because this was a specific *GQ* car. So the initial sketches were not too far away from the finished design – keeping it stronger and more confident. We didn't want a car for the mass market. We wanted a car for *GQ*.

THE PROTOTYPE – by Mark Lloyd, Citroën Chief Designer

From the original sketches, what we had was more of a 'wedge' design, which seemed as if it was trying a bit too hard. The tail was higher, the nose was lower...and it wasn't quite right. So to get rid of that angularity, we brought the nose up and made the front more generous and noble. We also rounded off the back, but retained the sculpted rear windscreen and the strong lines. And we retained the elements that define this as a Citroën: the long wheelbase, the hydraulic suspension, the interior comfort and space, the lightness of the controls.

As the design evolved, we also developed the idea of a rear suicide door. Something Citroën always tries to do is to create a dynamic between different design elements, for example, between small cars (such as the 2CV) and big cars (such as the DS), but in this case the contrast was between the front and the rear. So although we wanted this to be a sporty shooting brake, we contrasted that with the practical element of having a rear door.

The proportions on this car are really something special. Every line is justified by a function, we have the classic Citroën concave styling – in this case, on the rear window – and I really like the nose of this car in that it has a strong face, but the lower grilles turn the mouth into a smile. And those vents aren't just for show, they have a function. This is a car that is relaxed...it is at ease with itself, as the *GQ* man should be. It doesn't have complexes. It is proud and it doesn't want to be something it isn't. It's authentic.

As with *GQ*, this car fits extremely well with current attitudes. It is understated rather than in-your-face, sleek rather than too macho. And by using the skills of a Savile Row tailor to collaborate on the interior, we were further creating that bespoke, fitted feel.

All great cars create desire. They're not just functional or practical, they have a shape that provides pleasure. Great car design, as with art, creates an emotional response. We've achieved that here. Could it work, could it exist as a production vehicle? Why not?

THE INTERIOR – by Patrick Grant, Creative Director, Norton & Sons, Savile Row

When I first saw the designs for the *GQ* by Citroën, I was struck by how sleek and streamlined the exterior was. I realized the interior had to be equally unfussy. In search of inspiration, I noticed an old army uniform we had in the workroom at E Tautz. It was made for the commander-in-chief of the 4th Queen's Own Hussars, the regiment Winston Churchill would then have been serving in, and its red and black colour scheme was perfect for the Citroën's interior.

The cloth I used for the upholstery comes from a mill in Pudsey, West Yorkshire, called Hainsworth, which still provides the cloth for many British regiments. This is the mill that supplies the material known as doeskin, which has an amazing feel and is so called because it is almost as smooth as leather. It is felted, brushed, rolled, dipped, boiled and pressed repeatedly in a process that takes eight days, and the result is amazing: soft yet hard-wearing enough to see it through the wars – literally. This devotion to quality is why it is still made in the UK.

My next inspiration was a picture of Prince William laying a wreath at the Cenotaph in the uniform of The Household Cavalry. I wanted to reproduce the flash of red on the seats. Guardsmen in their bearskins were another inspiration, as the effect of the silver buttons against their jackets reminded me of the detailing on the *GQ* by Citroën's bucket seats.

And that was it. I was determined to keep it simple, just to complement it with leather detailing on the steering wheel and gear stick. What could be better than combining Savile Row heritage and French engineering to come up with something timelessly stylish?

THE END RESULT – by Jason Barlow, *GQ* Car Columnist

Geopolitics has conspired to turn Citroën into 2010's definitive car company. Why? Because qualities such as comfort, ecology and visual entertainment are arguably now more relevant than how fast a car goes or how well it takes a corner. Citroën has always specialized in the former, while generally ignoring the latter. There's a relaxed confidence to the brand, which, even in its darkest days, has always appealed to the more free-thinking car enthusiast.

The GQ by Citroën taps into this perfectly and caps a creative renaissance for a company that has unleashed the most spectacular wave of concept design studies in the past five years – the C-Métisse, GT by Citroën, C-Cactus, Hypnos and Revolte have all thoroughly reconnected Citroën with its brave back catalogue. ('Study all the possibilities, including the impossible,' Citroën's wartime vice-president Pierre Boulanger instructed his team. The incomparable DS was the result.) Good car design is about stance and proportion, and seeks to balance lots of competing visual elements with ever-tightening legislative demands. A quick glance at the GQ by Citroën is enough to confirm it as the work of people at the top of their game.

The GQ by Citroën exudes restrained confidence, despite the strong graphics and clever visual hooks. The front is almost vampiric, and cleverly evolves the racier elements premiered on the wild C-Métisse and Hypnos into something more plausible. As chief designer Mark Lloyd says, it's noble rather than macho. A rear suicide door and the concave back window add the necessary flourishes.

Sensuality is important to the French, and this car's body-sides have a voluptuous quality. But unlike the Italians, who reserve extreme beauty for their most exotic products, the GQ by Citroën is a car combining fitness for purpose with the sort of easy elegance that harks back to a time when travelling – and driving – was still a romantic gesture.

The horror of modern air travel might well revive that idea. With its memorable exterior and entertaining interior, the GQ by Citroën is certainly more bespoke than Ryanair. And with its plug-in hybrid engine it will be a lot more efficient, too.

Mercedes-McLaren SLR Stirling Moss
Reborn to be wild

The SLR Stirling Moss captured the spirit of motorsport's fearless Fifties.

ENGINE
5.4-litre supercharged V8, 650bhp

PERFORMANCE
0–62mph in 3.5 secs; top speed 217mph

YEAR OF DESIGN
2009

PRICE
£700,000 (approx.) ($1 million)

Car companies will try all sorts of unconscionable tricks when it comes to flogging a model that's reached the end of the road. My personal favourite remains 1998's Nissan Micra 'Wave' special edition that, if memory serves, had some eye-wateringly bad surf graphics and a free sunroof chucked in to sweeten the pill.

The new Mercedes-McLaren SLR Stirling Moss is limited to just 75 units, but it doesn't have a sunroof. In fact, it doesn't have a roof of any kind, in homage to the epochal mid-Fifties Mercedes-Benz 300 SLR, which survives intact in the Mercedes-Benz Museum, Stuttgart, and is said to be the world's most valuable car (worth £30 million/$44 million).

Provenance is all. Car No. 722 was the one Stirling Moss, regularly cited as the greatest driver in the history of motorsport, raced to victory in the 1955 Mille Miglia. Back then, road races were all the rage, especially in Italy, and the Mille Miglia (1,000 miles) was the sternest test of a driver's skill and sheer machismo. Moss and his navigator, Denis Jenkinson, won the race in a frankly terrifying 10 hours, 7 minutes, averaging 98.5mph across those 1,000 utterly unpredictable road miles. Of the 529 races Moss contested in his glorious but sadly abbreviated career (he crashed horribly at Goodwood in 1962 and opted to retire), this is his most celebrated.

The new car is a fitting tribute. Given that each of these 75 cars costs approximately £700,000 ($1 million), the aim is for this to be the ultimate incarnation of the Merc-Mac SLR collaborative effort that began back in 2003 with the launch of the original Coupé. Dramatically styled, sensationally engineered and constructed, the SLR nevertheless couldn't quite decide whether it wanted to be a bruising supercar or a golf-club toting super GT. The Stirling Moss special edition settles that debate. Say goodbye to the golf clubs...

Charging more for less is another car-industry ruse, but in this case less is, if not more, then certainly better. The SLR SM's engineers wanted the car to be 200kg (441lb) lighter than the Coupé, and to increase its top speed to a nice round 350kph (a less round 217mph, but I'm not complaining). So the roof, A-pillars and windscreen have all gone, creating a car that is both impressively minimalist and outrageously extrovert. The interior has been stripped, with lots of exposed carbon fibre, huge sills to clamber over and little in the way of gadgety distraction once you're inside.

Of course, you could argue that the car itself is one big sexy gadget. And the view from the driver's seat is extraordinary – elemental as well as just plain mental. The SLR SM uses the same 650bhp 5.4-litre supercharged V8 as 2006's 722 special edition, and also runs that car's uncompromising suspension geometry. The new car has a revised side-exhaust system, so given that the standard Coupé was one of the most outrageous-sounding bits of transport this side of Darth Vader's TIE Fighter, this signing-off special may well come with a health warning. We'll take our chances...

Mercedes-Benz C111
Wings of desire

Meet Mercedes' legendary C111, one of the most influential concept cars of the past 40 years. GQ *took off in this space-race classic and found it as comfortable on the catwalk as it was on the road.*

Mercedes' adventures with gull-wing doors span the epochal Fifties 300 SL and 2014's mighty SLS. But there was a third model, a car with a mystical resonance for Mercedes diehards, or fans of Seventies concept cars. The C111 sits alongside the likes of Pininfarina's Ferrari Modulo and Bertone's Stratos Zero and Carabo as the king of car design at its most wildly expressionist. Every creative in the business will have pictures of these things on a mood board somewhere. But the Mercedes is different.

The C111 first appeared at the 1969 Frankfurt Motor Show, barely seven weeks after the first moon landing and looking like a vehicle that could repeat the feat. Far from being a piece of eye candy, it was a functioning experimental prototype powered by a radical rotary engine that posited a whole new approach to internal combustion.

In 1970, a further four were made, with various other iterations sprinkled throughout the next few years. In fact, a total of 14 would be made in all. Having abandoned the tricky rotary unit for a turbocharged diesel, Mercedes also installed its silky 3.5-litre V8 into a C111 at some point in the early Seventies, a car that starred in a film promoting Berlin Fashion Week in 2015 and upstaged all of the models (and designers) on show – not just with its orange-over-black-retro-futuristic magnificence, but by being a proper runner. We can verify this, because we've driven it, and not just round the block at walking pace. For a concept car that is nearly 50 years old, the C111 is frankly astonishing, as thoroughly engineered as any other Mercedes of the period – and this at a time when its cars could rival Fort Knox for impregnability. Those wild doors and swooping body panels are the real knockout, and the interior has the hyperreal atmosphere Stanley Kubrick nailed so expertly in *A Clockwork Orange* (1971).

But true to its experimental remit, the C111's rear suspension featured a new setup that would find its way into the next generation of Mercedes road cars. So it actually handles beautifully, riding and gliding over typically choppy British country roads with unexpected aplomb.

It's also pretty fast, and its gearbox has a surprisingly treacly smooth action. In fact, the biggest threat to its wellbeing is likely to come from a learner driver in a Honda, so reluctantly we ease off. The C111 is insured for £6 million, but its real value is incalculable. And deserved.

ENGINE
2.4-litre 4-rotor, 350bhp
PERFORMANCE
0–62mph in 4.9 secs;
top speed 186mph
YEAR OF DESIGN
1970

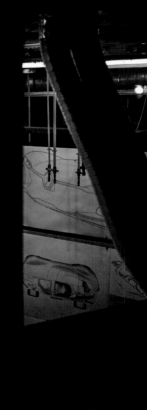

Renault Trezor
Trezor sharp

With groundbreaking design inside and out, Renault's new electric concept gave GQ a glimpse of a beautifully autonomous future.

French car giant Renault was suffering creative stasis when new design director Laurens van den Acker was appointed in 2009. Reimagining the entire visual language for a car company is a Herculean task, but he managed it and the Trezor ushers in phase two. An advanced carbon-fibre chassis underpins its swooping bodywork, but the real kicker is the Trezor's all-electric powertrain. Renault has been one of the prime movers in the Formula E race series since its inception in 2014, and the company is also Europe's bestselling electric vehicle manufacturer. So the Trezor's 260kW, 350hp motor is battle-hardened and, because electric power units deliver all their torque from a standstill, it will rocket to 62mph in less than four seconds.

The Trezor's exterior channels some of the most influential car designs of all time: Jaguar's XKSS and Pininfarina's 1970 Modulo, among others. Its body is covered in tiny little hexagons that change form as they flow into the car's curves. There are no A-pillars, so the screen wraps around in an uninterrupted flow, like the visor on a helmet.

Yet wood is also a major structural element; there's a naturally finished wooden frame under the vast bonnet that houses sumptuous leather luggage. The occupants access the cabin via a massive single-piece canopy, which hinges forward on flawlessly engineered struts. Inside, the analogue and digital face-off continues, and though the Trezor's lipstick-red cabin has a reconfigurable OLEO instrument panel, saddle leather and plump carpet are old-school luxury signifiers.

'I think it's a beautiful object,' van den Acker says. 'We're a popular brand, and we need to make cars that are easy to like.'

ENGINE
260kW electric motor, 350hp
PERFORMANCE
0–62mph in under 4 secs; top speed 155mph
YEAR OF DESIGN
2016

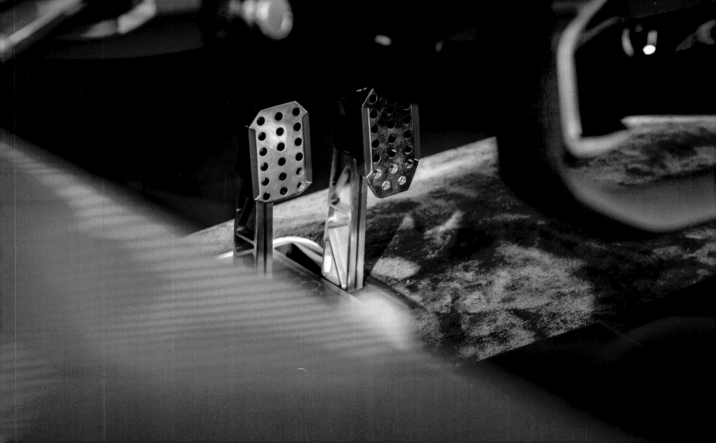

Honda FCX Clarity
Fuel desire

Forget International Rescue, Honda will save the world with its hydrogen-powered FCX Clarity. Well, maybe...

This, according to Honda, is the future of motoring. But it's not what is on the outside that counts; it's the neat little hand-built V-flow hydrogen fuel cell that powers a lightweight lithium-ion battery that matters. It creates 134bhp, taking the car from 0–62mph in ten seconds up to a top speed of 100mph, and on a full tank of premium hydrogen gives the FCX a range of 350 miles. Even better than that, the only by-product is water.

So that's it then. The ice caps will freeze up again, British summers will continue to be appalling and the receding ozone layer will get a comb-over. Well, almost.

Just like the planet-saving super-marionettes from the Sixties, there are a few strings attached. First, the fuel cell itself costs more than the average Premiership footballer. And, second, although hydrogen is the most plentiful substance in the universe, generating it in vast quantities in a green, economically viable way is some way off. And third, thanks to the cell and hydrogen tank and lithium battery, at the moment the FCX weighs almost as much as Thunderbird 2 would if it were real and made of lead.

Oh, and it's not cheap, either. 'As there are only two of these prototypes at the moment, if you were putting a value on them, it would certainly run into millions of pounds,' says Honda environmental manager John Kingston. So although Honda have talked about the possibility of going into limited production in America and Japan sometime, you won't actually be able to buy an FCX in the UK. The plan is you lease one and Honda will be able to monitor how it works.

What Honda has done is to put a lot of time, money and expertise into creating a viable alternative to the combustion engine. And what it has at the moment is a car that drives like a 'normal' car (albeit a bulky one). It runs almost silently, save for a mild whine as you put your foot down and the odd gurgle as water is expelled from the cell. Inside, from the space-age 'powerball' dial to the Bio-fabric eco seats that are sun- and stain-resistant, it looks and feels like a luxury vehicle. Give Honda another ten or fifteen years and you might just be reading about the hydrogen car of the year. That's if the Mysterons don't take over the world first. In summary then, the Honda FCX is FAB.

ENGINE
Vertical hydrogen fuel cell stack

PERFORMANCE
0–62mph in 10 secs; top speed 100mph (electronically limited... it could go faster)

YEAR OF DESIGN
2007

PRICE
Somewhere between £2–10 million ($4–20 million)

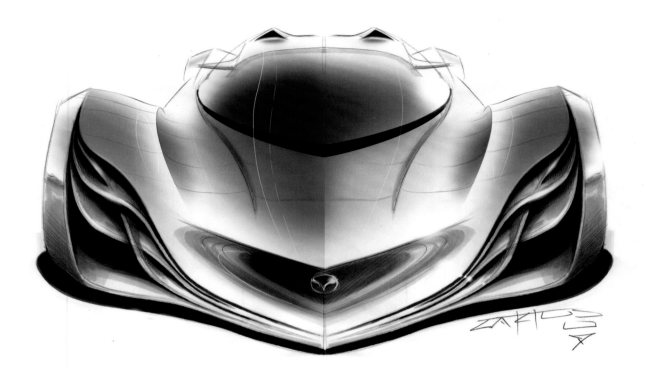

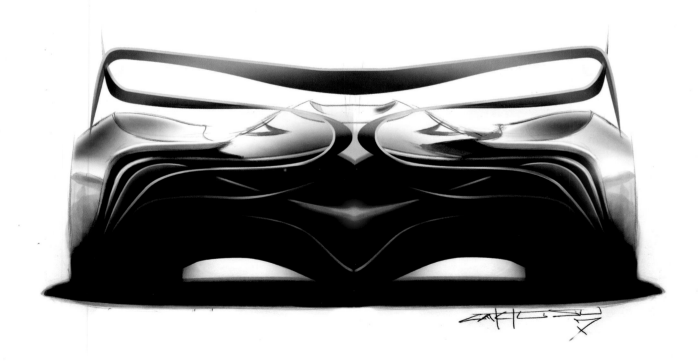

Mazda Furai
The fast and the furai

Mazda's stealth-like Furai, inspired by the 'sound of the wind', was a breath of fresh air in contemporary car design.

Laurens van den Acker and Franz von Holzhausen sound like 19th-century European noblemen, but they're actually the crown princes of contemporary car design. Van den Acker, for example, has overseen a series of Mazda concept cars so visually powerful that his boss, Ford creative director J Mays, says it has 'finally unlocked the secrets of Japanese design'.

The Nagare, Ryuga, Kabura and Taiki have taken inspiration from *nagare* – Japanese for 'natural flow'. Wind, air, rain, storm fronts, this is weather forecasting as car design. The idea has been so well received that the series of four cars has been extended to five with von Holzhausen's sensational Furai.

The Furai is pretty much a full-blown racing car, based on a Courage chassis as used in the American Le Man Series (ALMS), and harks back to the endurance racers of the Eighties and Nineties. 'We needed to elevate awareness of Mazda's motorsport success,' says Von Holzhausen.

Its body generates impressive downforce, and the flamboyant slats and bodywork grooves funnel air in the right direction for aero and cooling purposes. The airbox above the passenger cell splits air in two directions, feeding the clean stuff to the 450bhp mid-mounted rotary engine and filtering the less efficient air and debris. The Furai uses a six-speed sequential transmission that can apparently handle up to 750bhp.

All this begs the question: is Mazda gearing up for another assault on Le Mans? 'I hope so, man,' says Van den Acker.

ENGINE
2.0-litre triple-rotor, 450bhp
PERFORMANCE
0–62mph in 3.2 secs; top speed 172mph
YEAR OF DESIGN
2007

Chapter 5
Made in America

It would be easy to sum up the American automotive industry in two words: muscle cars. Ferocious V8 engines delivering tonnes of torque in a straight line, followed by disastrous consequences in the corner. But that would be to miss the point of the finest American motors, because for all their big-block brutality and questionable handling, there is something irresistible about these monumental slabs of steel. And then there are the names...the Ford Mustang, Chevrolet Corvette, Dodge Challenger. If those cars don't instantly make you think of Steve McQueen in *Bullitt*, the *Fast & Furious* movies or *Vanishing Point*, sorry, but you are reading the wrong book. If, however, modern muscle cars aren't your thing, don't worry because we have something rather special in this chapter just for you. How about an American racing car that can handle the bends as well as anything on four wheels, and happens to be made by Ford? You're welcome. And have a nice day.

Ford Mustang Bullitt
One not-so-careful owner

GQ tracked down the original Ford Mustang as driven by the legendary Steve McQueen in Bullitt...*just in time to celebrate the new 50th anniversary version.*

ORIGINAL MUSTANG

ENGINE
4,946cc V8, 325bhp

PERFORMANCE
0–62mph in 5.5 secs;
top speed 140mph

YEAR OF RELEASE
1968

PRICE ON RELEASE
$2,900 (approx.)

2018 MUSTANG

ENGINE
5,038cc V8, 458bhp

PERFORMANCE
0–62mph in 4.6 secs;
top speed 163mph

YEAR OF RELEASE
2018

PRICE ON RELEASE
£47,545 (approx.)
($45,000)

The car chase in *Bullitt* (1970) is the stuff of legend, with the Highland Green Mustang Fastback possibly the most revered movie car of all. Warner Bros bought two. Word was, one was lost in Mexico somewhere. The other? Who knew.

Well, I'm sitting in it right now, barely able to believe it. This is the car that enjoyed 90 per cent of the screen time, while the other 'jump' car did the really hard yards. Gluey traces on the rev counter betray a sticker placed there advising the movie's star not to over-rev the big-block V8. Can't imagine he paid much attention. There's no head lining inside, the wood trim is faded and the bodywork even has patches of corrosion. In old car parlance, this Mustang is heavily 'patinated', but we're practically inhaling Steve McQueen here.

Its owner is Nashville-based Sean Kiernan. 'For 40 years,' he says, 'it was a total secret.' Kiernan's father, who had been chasing a Mustang with the 390-cubic-inch, big-block engine, found one for sale in the classified section of *Road & Track* magazine. 'October 1974 issue,' says Kiernan. 'It was incorrectly advertised as the "Bullet" car. I think my dad paid about $4,000 for it.'

A full rebuild was started in 2014 and the car's now worth around £3 million ($3.8 million). It sounds spectacular and it's as beautifully gnarly as only late-1960s US muscle cars can be. But its imperfections are what make it so utterly extraordinary. 'The camera mounts under it are ugly welded things. There's another on the left front that's welded over the fuel line and a weld on a bumper bracket. There's a hole in the trunk for the smoke machine. The reason the car has a new bumper, coincidentally, is because my grandfather backed into it twice.'

McQueen would probably have laughed. As an irredeemable petrolhead, he personally cast the Mustang. Fifty years on, his co-star is making something approaching a comeback...although, like so many aging Hollywood stars, it has had an awful lot of work done.

The Mustang reboot has been given what Ford calls the 'Bullitt special-edition treatment'. The modifications are modest, but more than enough. The 5.0-litre V8 is being nudged towards a 458bhp power output, thanks to a larger throttle body and revised intake manifold and, as on the original, this old-school grunt is funnelled to the road via a six-speed manual transmission, complete with a cue-ball-topped shifter. (McQueen was not an automatic kind of man.)

It has upgraded suspension, bigger brakes and racy Michelin Pilot Sport tyres. Exterior revisions run to black magnesium wheels, minimal badging, a 'Dark Highland Green' paint job and a retro fuel-filler cap. An active performance exhaust with 'Black Nitro' tips is an option, as are magnetic dampers.

Standard interior equipment includes a 30cm (12-inch) all-digital LCD instrument cluster, featuring a unique Bullitt welcome screen that fires up in green with an image of the car rather than the pony. The Bang & Olufsen audio system features a dual-voice coil subwoofer for deep bass and delivers 1,000 watts of audio power through 12 high-performance speakers. The standard seats feature green stitching, and Mustang Bullitt customers can choose black leather-trimmed Recaro sports seats.

'Nothing captured the spirit and excitement of Mustang quite like that amazing car chase in *Bullitt*,' Steven Armstrong, group vice president and president of Europe, Middle East and Africa, Ford Motor Company, says. 'The new Mustang Bullitt will pack a similar punch with more power, high specification and – just like the film's star – dripping with understated cool.'

Even better than the real thing? Maybe...maybe not.

Chevrolet Corvette Z06/Z07
The American dream

What began in 1953 as a jet-age sports car had by 2015 evolved into an extreme machine. GQ *tried to tame the Chevrolet Corvette Z06.*

ENGINE
6.2-litre supercharged V8, 650bhp

PERFORMANCE
0–62mph in 2.95 secs (Z07 automatic); top speed 200+mph

YEAR OF RELEASE
2014

PRICE ON RELEASE
£99,140 ($78,995)

'Junior Johnson has followers who need to keep him, symbolically, riding through the nighttime like a demon. [He] is one of the last of those sports stars who is not just an ace at the game itself, but a hero a whole people or class of people can identify with.'

In his celebrated 1965 piece for *Esquire* magazine, Tom Wolfe's breathless, deathless tumbling prose nailed the appeal of America's nascent stock-car-racing scene. Men like Johnson had been moonshine runners and had fought but mostly dodged the law in their modified Fords and Chevrolets. Junior ran a hot rod with a 'one-brake' wheel; he could spin the thing 180 degrees in a heartbeat for a quick getaway. His skills later enabled him to trade his outlaw status for NASCAR glory.

The US muscle car has its roots in this arcane automotive Americana. While European interlopers such as Ferrari, Jaguar and Porsche wooed Hollywood's new princes, the American everyman – soon to be hymned by Bruce Springsteen – got his hands dirty with the Buick Riviera, Chevy Camaro SS, Dodge Charger, Ford Mustang and Pontiac GTO. These were blue-collar supercars, technically crude but fast, fun, easy to tinker with and, most of all, affordable. They had the whiff of moonshine about them.

Chevrolet's Corvette was different. It began life in 1953 as a sports car that mixed priapic styling flourishes with the jet-age affectations of the era. By the time it had morphed into the Stingray a decade later, the party could really begin. Each successive 'Vette accurately mirrored the American Age: the Coke-bottle-waisted Seventies iteration matched the coke-addled, wasted *Boogie Nights* era; the slinky modernism of the Eighties car would have chimed with Richard Gere's *American Gigolo* if only his Armani apparel hadn't been better suited to a Mercedes SL.

Now this American idol, like everything, faces challenges from unexpected sources in our atomized culture. But there's no faded glory: in its Z06 guise, this Corvette is so idiomatically awesome it bludgeons all-comers. Look beyond the long hood/short tail and there's a lot of nuanced aerodynamic detail. In fact, one thing the Corvette has done brilliantly for years is prove its mettle in brutal endurance events like the Le Mans 24 Hours. So while the Z06 base model is primarily a road car, it can handle the rigours of a track.

To which end, it comes with some pretty special options: a 'level two' package adds a front diffuser with end plates, and a rear wing. Go to 'level three', though, and you get an even more pronounced aero setup, semi-slick Michelin Pilot Super Sport Cup tyres, Brembo carbon-ceramic brakes and a very trick rear spoiler. Chevy also had to level up the name – this one's called the Z07, suggesting confidence bordering on hubris.

As does letting us loose on one of America's most notorious circuits: Road Atlanta, Georgia. A fearsome mix of blind crests, downhill esses and a flat-out back straight, this is one of those tracks where physics asks a car to do two opposing things simultaneously. If you're on the power or the brakes too long or in the wrong place, you're in trouble. It's a phenomenal challenge.

But the track-modified Z07 is a phenomenal car. Its chassis is a hydroformed aluminium spaceframe, so it's stiff but also light. At its heart sits a 6.2-litre supercharged V8, with rotocast aluminium cylinder heads, titanium intake valves and machined connecting rods. This produces 650bhp and 650lb ft of torque, the sort of numbers that would have had Junior Johnson choking on his 'shine. Chevy's manual gearbox can cope with the immense forces this amount of grunt generates, though there's an old-school auto, too.

The driving position is low-slung, the windscreen sufficiently narrow to flood your senses with another Tom Wolfe allusion, this time *The Right Stuff* (1979). A heads-up display beams all the key info into your line of vision, reinforcing the fighter-pilot aspiration, and there's a performance-data recorder, analysing and saving your lap time onto an SD card for dissemination. One wonders what Chuck Yeager would have made of YouTube.

The 'Vette would certainly have blown his mind. The Z07 is unquestionably one of the craziest, airiest, greatest cars I've ever experienced. Its performance is on the unhinged side of extreme – anything that can hit 60mph in under three seconds is automatically a member of an elite club. It would be easy to assume that it's all about straight-line urge, but the Z06/7 is actually packing some sophisticated chassis electronics. A drive-mode selector gives you five settings that monitor twelve variables, including throttle input, suspension and the car's electronic differential.

In other words, it's programmed to curb your enthusiasm, or fill in the talent vacuum, and on the track it means that you can take almost diabolical liberties with all 650 of those horses. Set to 'track' mode, there are five levels of torque reduction and braking stability, and it's been so expertly configured that even racing drivers don't moan about it stifling their fun. If anything, the way it brakes from 150mph to 30 is even more sensational than the way it accelerates. At one point, we pull 1.54g (gravity), which is heart-stopping stuff in a road car.

And on the road itself? It's a pussycat. That mighty V8 has been designed to ply the freeway on four of its eight cylinders, its crank spinning lazily while you surf Sirius XM for a soundtrack. It's so good Whitesnake works in this thing.

Jeep Grand Cherokee & Chevrolet Camaro Coupe Reborn in the USA

GQ raced to the state line (well, the border of Buckinghamshire) in two American muscle cars with 6.0-litre engines and an eco-conscience.

JEEP GRAND CHEROKEE SRT8

The American diner (opposite) is not on Sunset or in Phoenix, or even Arkansas. No, this faux fast-food experience is brought to you courtesy of the A40 heading out of London, well beyond the Westway, as hymned by The Clash, and closer to the Polish War Memorial, and therefore as unprepossessing a stretch of road as you'll find anywhere. For all its lack of geographical authenticity, though, Starvin' Marvin's fries and shakes taste pretty good. You could level similar charges of contextual inappropriateness at the Jeep Grand Cherokee SRT8. Are we for real?

The American car industry – with mighty Detroit the fulcrum on which it turned – nearly came a cropper 45 years ago when the Yom Kippur War triggered an oil shock. Almost overnight, America's land yachts and her domestic consumers' lust for them impaled the entire business on its own arrogance, and millions of people threw themselves headlong into Honda Civics instead. But if there's one thing we know, it's that history teaches us nothing.

How else can you explain a two-tonne-plus American 'performance' SUV? That, surely, is the question only the planet's most misguided misanthrope and vehement climate-change denier could be asking.

Owned by Chrysler, once one of Motown's totemic brands, the machinations of 21st-century business now finds the company under the Fiat umbrella. An odd coupling it may be, but the signs are that it's working. The regular Cherokee is a fine vehicle, but in SRT8 form it's borderline startling. It sits an inch lower, has swollen wheel-arches, fantastic 20in-forged alloy wheels, a new single-piece a colossal front spoiler and Brembo brakes with discs the size of man-hole covers. The whole thing is unequivocally steroidal, but stays the right side of lobotomized.

The engine is a 6.4-litre V8, with hemispherical combustion chambers, and 470bhp. This is a fair bit, even for a lump of metal this heavy. But despite my deep-seated reservations, this is no old-school American iron. Ninety per cent of the SRT8's thumping 465lb ft of torque – that's the stuff that gives an engine its kick-in-the-back shove – comes on stream from 2,800rpm, a relatively modest crank speed, and stays there until 6,000rpm. This makes it twice as

JEEP GRAND CHEROKEE SRT8

ENGINE
6.4-litre hemi V8, 461bhp
PERFORMANCE
0–62mph in 5 secs;
top speed 160mph
YEAR OF RELEASE
2012
PRICE ON RELEASE
£58,995 ($55,295)

effective as the outgoing 6.1-litre hemi engine, and also means that forward progress is so vivid that if you bury your right foot, you can seriously intimidate your passengers and other road users. Stop acting like a moron, and the SRT8's engine shuts off four of its eight cylinders, and behaves respectably and almost economically.

It would still be a pointless party trick if the rest of the Jeep had the dynamic poise of a storm-tossed Newfoundland fishing vessel, which is absolutely what I expected. But it's a whopping 146 per cent stiffer than the old Jeep Cherokee, and has an active damping system that's in constant dialogue with other parts of the chassis, so the upshot is a car that handles amazingly well, should you start probing the outer reaches of sanity. For the record, it'll do 160mph, which is a bit daft in all honesty but endearing.

In fact, by the time I returned it to *GQ* HQ via a warren of London side streets, the Cherokee SRT8 had fair demolished all my preconceptions. It should be rubbish, really, but even its seats are good, trimmed in tactile nappa leather and Alcantara, while its major controls are full of a weighty positivity.

Yes, it likes a drink. But then, so did Ernest Hemingway.

THE CHEVY CAMARO

Remember the marshmallow test? An ingenious little willpower study conducted on schoolchildren in the Sixties, in which hundreds of four-year-olds were left in a room with a marshmallow and told they could either eat the treat now or hold out for another 15 minutes and have two? American kids didn't do so well. Delayed gratification was an oxymoronic concept in America then – and 50-odd years on, nothing's changed. Unlike Brits, Yanks want their painkillers to kill pain, taps to run hot and cold, and cars to be functional. They want the marshmallow now.

Living in America has made me just as impatient. I've lost a taste for the finer, subtler things and developed an appreciation for the immediate and the infallible. Which is why the new Chevrolet Camaro is my kind of car. When news broke a few years ago that General Motors was thinking of ditching the 'Chevy' nickname, there was an angry outpouring. GM rushed to clarify its original memo: you don't mess with success. And when Snoop Dogg raps about

a car, ('When I'm ridin' in my Chevy and I'm sittin' at the light...') it's well and truly embedded in the social psyche.

In its youth, the Chevy was slender and wide-hipped. Now that it's had children (and grandchildren) this, the 45th Anniversary Camaro, has lost its streamlined physique and settled into the boxy, efficient body of a middle-aged mother of three. The Carbon Flash exterior and rally stripes are still there, along with new 20in dark-silver wheels, a spoiler and HID (high-intensity discharge) headlights, but this Camaro with a 'mummy cut' no longer relies on its looks to make the grade.

Powering down the motorway outside London, I may not be attracting the kind of attention of a first- or second-generation Camaro, but the new 6.2 V8 engine more than makes up for the lack of ogling. It's fuel-efficient (Chevy insists it's good for 30mpg) and with its firm six-speed manual gearshift and lighter carcass (thanks to a new composite, the car's lost weight) the Camaro's the kind of car you want to speed, if not Hunter S Thompson-like through Death Valley, then at least along the A40, with a quick pit stop at Starvin' Marvin's.

Now I'm all for Americana, but rather like the Fifties-inspired motorway diner, the Anniversary Camaro has the unfortunate downside of looking like the US of A threw up all over it – after a three-course dinner consisting entirely of stars-and-stripes-iced cake. The dashboard instrument panel, steering wheel and sill plates are splattered with logos, while red, white and blue stitching lines the centre console, seats and armrests. Nostalgia, it occurs to me as I wash down a hot dog with an Oreo Cookie Shake and stick Don McLean on the jukebox, can all too often stick in your throat.

Forty-five is a tricky age. Your life is essentially over but a part of you still yearns for excitement. You could have picked up the new Camaro for £35,025 ($32,280), the £25 ($39) will get you a boot full of marshmallows, which you can down all in one) and enjoy its new power and economy; or you could wait five years for what's bound to be a more distinguished model. Because let's face it, 50 is easier to celebrate. Your life may be over, but you've accepted it and embarked on the final furlong with grace.

THE CHEVROLET CAMARO

ENGINE
6.2-litre V8

PERFORMANCE
0–62mph in 5.2 secs;
top speed 155mph

YEAR OF RELEASE
2012

PRICE ON RELEASE
£35,025 ($32,280)

Ford GT
There's a Ford in your future

Fifty years after Ford's legendary supercar swept the board at Le Mans, the GT returned to claim its crown, and the street version was even hotter than the racer...

In 1966, Ford scored one of the great sporting routs of all time. Having tried – and failed – to buy Ferrari, Henry Ford II vowed to hit the flinty, demagogic Enzo Ferrari where he knew it would really hurt: on the racetrack. Nine times Ferrari had triumphed in the world's greatest endurance race, the Le Mans 24 Hours, but in 1966, Ford's brutally beautiful GT40 endurance racer crushed the Italians in spectacular style. In fact, Ford was so dominant the team was able to choreograph a perfect 1-2-3 finish.

Now the GT is back, in road car form and as a competition machine. As well as competing in FIA World Endurance Championship (WEC) and the US-focused IMSA series, Ford's plan was to build 250 road-going GT supercars per year. 'The GT represents everything that is great at Ford,' Dave Pericak, Ford Performance global director, says.

'When Henry Ford II said, "Go get it," and rolled out all the resources and they actually did get it...well, we're doing that again now. We've got the right product, the right team, the right drivers with the right heart and the ability to dig that little bit deeper...'

The 2016 WEC driver line-up included British endurance stars Andy Priaulx and Marino Franchitti and would race against Aston Martin, Corvette, Ferrari and Porsche at venues such as Spa, Silverstone and the Nürburgring, as well as Le Mans. For motorsport fans, this was akin to putting the band back together, albeit reborn in an ultra-high-tech guise. American racing blue blood Chip Ganassi was charged with running the race team and he wasn't about to settle for second. 'If you're a team owner in sport – any sport – what do you get out of it if you're not winning? There's really very little reason to get in an accident in a 24-hour race. I tell my drivers, "If you hit someone, obviously it's your fault. If someone hits you, it's your fault. The only time it's possibly not your fault is if a meteor falls from space and lands on your car."'

What Ford gets is the opportunity to develop an all-new, highly evolved supercar in parallel with a competition car. 'When we put the road car next to the race car, other than some items, such as the fixed wing, they are the same car,' Pericak says. 'I'll repeat – it's the same car. We're thrilled to be racing again and it's a huge deal for the company. But the GT road car is really more important in this whole story for Ford: it serves the brand globally.'

ENGINE
3.5-litre twin-turbo EcoBoost V6, 647bhp
PERFORMANCE
0–62mph in 3 secs; top speed 216mph
YEAR OF RELEASE
2016
PRICE ON RELEASE
£450,000 ($456,950)

The street GT version is powered by the same 3.5-litre, twin-turbo EcoBoost V6 as the race car but, thanks to the FIA's controversial 'Balance Of Performance' regulations, it'll actually be more powerful than its track sibling. Well over 600bhp, in fact, to go with that carbon-fibre chassis and highly aerodynamic body.

And Franchitti is certainly a fan. 'It goes even better than it looks, which is saying something,' he says. 'I was in tune with it immediately and that's not something that happens as often as you'd like. This isn't just marketing stuff. This is Ford in maximum attack mode.'

Dodge Challenger SRT8
Retro active

Dodge's refitted ride of 2008 was an absolute blast (from the past).

The best thing about 1971 countercultural classic *Vanishing Point* is a naked girl riding a motorcycle. The second best is the Dodge Challenger that Barry Newman's amphetamine-addled hero plunges into the jaws of a bulldozer.

Bereft of imagination it might be, but Dodge's refit of this back-catalogue muscle car wheel-spun its way to the top of my 2008 best cars list. Well, I say best, but what I really mean is memorable. Or possibly even just plain ridiculous. Whichever it is, it works.

Anyway, the new Challenger magically transcends its retro brief. The way it does this is quite simple: it's shockingly good to drive. Granted, I'd sooner have been heading north out of LA, 'American Woman' by The Guess Who blasting out of the stereo. But instead it was delivered to my house in the English countryside, scattering the ducks and worrying the neighbours. Nowhere for this giant, petrol-guzzling anomaly to hide round here – just twisty roads and old folk trundling to the pub at 37mph. It should have been a disaster.

The Challenger really is an epic-looking car. Almost identical outside to the 2006 concept that prefigured it, it distils all that's good about the past 40 years of American car design into one shape. It has a grille (modern cars don't have these any more), four simple headlights, a bonnet so long the front bumper has a different address to the rest of the car, and an upswept curvy bit over the rear wheel arch. Forget the Mini, Beetle, Fiat 500 or Ford Mustang: this is the best retro design of the lot.

The interior is mostly rubbish, with budget plastics and cabin trim that has all the tactile sophistication of an elephant's backside. Nor is the 6.1-litre hemi engine exactly state-of-the-art – though it is good for a hefty 425bhp and wears the best badge of any engine ever ('hemi' denotes the hemispherical shape of the combustion chamber).

But the Challenger is immensely entertaining. Taken to the cleaners dynamically by Europe and Japan's best, of course, but still sure-footed, controlled and comfortable to punt along at serious speeds. Most American cars are to tightening-radius corners what Nixon was to the truth, but this one is fluid and accurate. Good job, too, because when it comes to celebrated Detroit metal, there's nothing left worth ripping off. Vanishing point indeed...

ENGINE
6.1-litre hemi V8, 425bhp
PERFORMANCE
0–62mph in 4.9 secs;
top speed 174mph
YEAR OF RELEASE
2008
PRICE ON RELEASE
£39,000 ($37,320)

Chapter 6
Off-Road Warriors

As motor trends go, the rise and rise of the SUV (sports utility vehicle) has been nothing short of phenomenal. Once considered the automotive equivalent of lumbering dinosaurs, the 21st century has seen such an explosion in 4x4 demand that even the likes of Rolls-Royce, Bentley and Maserati have joined the off-road party. And, in truth, it is easy to see why they have become so popular. With an elevated driving position, new levels of luxury and refinement, plus safety standards other cars can only dream of, the modern SUV is the definitive urban family vehicle. But only the finest examples qualify for inclusion in *GQ Drives*, which is why we have chosen six of the best examples of the breed. These SUVs can all double happily as highway cruisers, but if we are going to get down and dirty, we want to do it in style because where we're going in these 4x4s, we don't need roads...

Audi Q8 S Line
Peak SUV? This might be it…

Off-road hulks with coupé poise are nothing new, but with the Audi Q8 the concept was given a major lift. And, in the thin skies above the Atacama, GQ found this fierce 4x4 to be a breath of fresh air.

ENGINE
3.0-litre V6, 282bhp
PERFORMANCE
0–62mph in 6.3 secs;
top speed 144mph
YEAR OF RELEASE
2018
PRICE ON RELEASE
£65,000 ($68,990)

How far would you go to test-drive a new car? If the answer is 'down to the local dealership in my lunch hour, if I wasn't too busy', you aren't really a car person. There's nothing wrong with that. Not everyone is. If you are a car person, though, you might be prepared to go a little further afield. And for the right car, well…you'd probably go almost anywhere.

Which is how *GQ* recently found itself in Chile's Atacama Desert – where James Bond experienced his *Quantum of Solace* (2008) – the driest non-polar region on Earth, shivering on a windswept, sand-blasted, rocky plateau 4,500m (14,760ft) above sea level, in the shadow of the Andes, suffering the early effects of altitude sickness.

And yet, despite the throbbing headache, nausea, heart palpitations and breathlessness, we couldn't help but smile. Not because we were experiencing onset drug-like delirium, but for one simple reason: we are car people and we were in the right car.

The Q8 is Audi's new flagship SUV, a 4x4 that has the squat, muscular presence of an off-roader with the sleek lines of a coupé. Audi isn't the first to come up with this design style – BMW's X6, Mercedes' GLE and, arguably, the Range Rover Velar arrived at the party a wee while ago – but the interlopers from Ingolstadt certainly know how to make an entrance.

For starters, it has had a major face-lift. The wide, aggressive grille is an eight-sided single-frame statement that, coupled with its narrowed LED headlamps, doesn't so much scream, 'Look at me!', as menacingly demand, 'What the hell are you looking at?' That 'want-some?' attitude continues on the Q8's flanks, with rippling flared wheel arches flattering four serious 21in wheels, and continues at the back, where a roof spoiler and flat rear end complete a body that tips more than a hat to the iconic 'Ur' Quattro of the Eighties.

'We didn't just take design cues from the Quattro,' says Mauricio Monteiro Dos Santos, one of Audi's lead project designers. 'Once you drive it, you will realize the Q8 also shares DNA with our legendary rally car.' Those are very big genetic shoes to fill.

On the inside, instead of a Quattro-inspired dash (you really wouldn't want that), you get a stark and stripped-back cockpit free of clutter, knobs and various vents. In their place are the elegant virtual dials and touchscreens familiar to Q7 and A5 drivers. Audi does interiors exceptionally well, and the Q8 is no exception. It might not be what you would call different, but if it ain't broke...

However, the best qualities of the Q8 are those you don't see. Instead, you can hear them (the Bang & Olufsen stereo is an audio monster in a near-silent cabin), feel them (the air suspension can handle any lump, bump or Chilean armadillo) and appreciate them (there are 39 driver assists, laser scanners and radars all beavering away to keep you pre-sense safe and sound) as you sit back and enjoy the views.

That said, while those views are truly incredible, they might not be worth suffering a high-altitude cerebral oedema for – not on a test drive that is, even if you are a car person.

Land Rover Discovery
Disco in the desert

The fifth-gen Discovery proved Land Rover's latest dune-busting SUV had found its calling, from highway to hinterland.

In the Coral Pink Sand Dunes in southwestern Utah, there's a beetle that you won't find anywhere else on the planet, earning a section of the dunes protected status and a cordon. How this little critter knows not to stray isn't clear, but today they're joined by a fleet of Land Rover Discoveries, individual tyre pressures reduced from 34 to just 18psi to lengthen their rubber footprint and generate the necessary purchase on the sand.

The dunes look magnificent, but there's real hostility in this terrain, at least if you're planning to point two tonnes of premium SUV down a constantly morphing landmass. Or, worse still, trying to drive up it. But the Discovery does it with ease, just as it can manage a rock crawl – also tricky, if not mechanically fatal, when tackled in the wrong car. It can do everything, this formidably engineered British masterpiece that dreams of a life beyond the shopping mall car park.

The fifth generation is all new and represents arguably the biggest overhaul in the Discovery's 30-year existence. Land Rover is a company transformed in that time, from former British Leyland basket case into one of the world's most coveted brands. If the Range Rover is the most complete luxury vehicle on sale, its little brother aspires to an all-encompassing usefulness. That's more relevant but not as sexy, which is probably why the new Disco has gone upmarket. This isn't a risk-free strategy, because a fully lockable differential is the beardy Land Rover loyalist's idea of connectivity and you can't operate a touchscreen with gloves on. So this car has it all to do.

The new Disco's body is 85 per cent aluminium, which cuts a thumping 454kg (1,000lb) off the base car's weight, and the entire body side is a single pressing to improve rigidity while being less complex to manufacture. There's another single-piece pressing for the floor, the dash structure is magnesium, and lightweight steel is used on the front and rear sub-frames. The air suspension has a state-of-the-art integral multilink rear to minimize roll without wrecking the ride, while still preserving the impact resistance an SUV needs.

At the heart of its incredible versatility is a software system called Terrain Response 2, which automatically monitors and optimizes throttle, steering and traction, while the All-Terrain Progress Control (ATPC) is effectively an off-road cruise control. Ground clearance of 283mm (11in) and wheel articulation of 500mm (20in) mean that even the most clod-hopping off-road neophyte can work magic.

ENGINE
2.0-litre, 4-cylinder, 240bhp
PERFORMANCE
0–62mph in 8.3 secs; top speed 121mph
YEAR OF RELEASE
2017
PRICE ON RELEASE
£43,495 ($50,895)

'We wanted to create a vehicle that was easy for as many people as possible to use,' chief product engineer Alex Heslop says. Even up a fast-flowing river, the Discovery has a 900mm (35in) wading depth, thanks to a 'labyrinth intake' system that basically means the engine can breathe underwater. 'It could go deeper,' Heslop tells me, 'but above that figure you lose traction at the rear and the car begins to float. And you need to open the rear doors to combat that, which isn't ideal.'

It's also peerless when it's not semi-aquatic. We switched between the 254bhp 3.0-litre TDV6 and 340bhp 3.0-litre Si6 petrol, both of which swept us through the imperious Utah landscape with minimum fuss. The smaller 2.0-litre diesel is much less refined, but still does a game job of hauling what is a very substantial car. The interior is endlessly configurable and accommodates seven full-size adults in total comfort. Between the giant door bins, glove box and underfloor areas, there's 172 litres (180 quarts) of storage, and four iPads or a pair of 2-litre (4-pint) water bottles can fit in the centre console. Up to four 12V sockets and nine USB charging points can be specified, and in-car 4G Wi-Fi can support up to eight devices.

The driver and passenger get Jaguar Land Rover's InControl Touch Pro multimedia setup, which includes a 10in touchscreen, dual view, satnav with a new 'commute mode' and all sorts of other displays and graphics. The Meridian audio system was treated to some serious drum'n'bass at one point (our co-driver was Brit rapper Example, not your average in-car DJ) and was powerful enough to dislodge chunks of 90-million-year-old canyon.

So, what we have here is a monumentally capable car. But there are a few issues. First, the outgoing Discovery's blocky modernism apparently polarized too many potential customers, although I personally regard it as a 21st-century design classic. The new one is smoother but more generic looking, and creating a space big enough for that third row of seats has saddled it with a hefty rear end. Second, the Disco's upmarket aspirations, though perfectly legitimate and attuned to the market, give it a distinctly different character. And cost...prices start at £43,495 ($50,895). We tested it to the point of destruction in some of the harshest terrain we could find, then went shopping in it, so we know it can cope. But we'd have ours with rubber floor mats.

Masserati Levante
The tailor-made SUV

Maserati's latest marriage of silk and steel was as theatrical as you would imagine, but the Levante also brought some unexpected utility to Italy's most individual and charismatic marque.

ENGINE
3.0-litre V6 turbo diesel,
271bhp
PERFORMANCE
0–62mph in 6.9 secs;
top speed 143mph
YEAR OF RELEASE
2016
PRICE ON RELEASE
£54,335 ($72,000)

Gildo Zegna, CEO of Ermenegildo Zegna, is talking fabric. 'Putting real silk in a car is a huge challenge. We wanted to create a cocoon-like feeling within the car while allowing the driver to experience all the comforts that a Maserati is known for.' Maserati's boss, the straight-talking German Harald Wester, is even more explicit. 'If you like this type of precious material, you don't only want to wear it. It's even more appealing to get into the car and drive it.'

Silk in a car: it's a very Maserati thing to do. And it really works. Woven at Zegna's Trivero mills, the limited-run Maserati Quattroporte uses 12m (13yd) of specially emboldened silk, four times the amount used in a two-piece suit, a highly tactile and visual enlivener of the seats, door inlays and the headlining. These are the bits of interior real estate that usually receive very little love.

The Zegna option is also available on Maserati's new SUV, the Levante. Purists, if they haven't all been beaten into submission by commercial realpolitik, would point to Maserati as the most fashionable and aristocratic of Italian car brands, the epitome of period Como chic more understated than Enzo Ferrari's slightly arriviste rival, and creator of arguably the greatest Grand Prix car ever in the shape of the Fifties 250F. Surely this is the last company that should be wading into the 4x4 market? But those same naysayers should also know that Maserati has flirted with fiscal disaster repeatedly during its 100-plus-year existence, and the only way to stay truly relevant – and profitable – is to give the people what they want.

And they want one of these. This, the company insists, is the 'Maserati of SUVs', a claim that could mean any number of things depending on how you feel about this most quixotic of Italian brands. Having spent some proper time in the Ghibli sports saloon, I can confirm that character goes a long way towards atoning for its dynamic failings, and that Maserati makes cars you can't help looking over your shoulder at when you've just parked up. Which is a more polite way of saying that the Ghibli doesn't quite fulfil its promise.

The Levante does, though. Maserati's design team is full of well-dressed young tyros overseen by the now semi-retired styling maestro Lorenzo Ramaciotti, and the Levante is a daring reinvention of the current design language. The grille and headlights are extraordinarily expressive, the glass area manages to preserve Maserati's inherent sportiness, and the upswept curve over the rear wheels evolves the cues used with mixed results on the Ghibli.

It's a big car – in excess of 5m (16ft) long – but manages to camouflage its bulk with more charisma than the rather lumpen Audi Q7 or amorphous Porsche Cayenne. Warning: it's colour-sensitive, and Maseratis, more than most cars, benefit from the appropriate context. White in Miami works, less so in Macclesfield.

Actually, think of the whole car as an evolved Ghibli and you're about there. It uses the same platform but feels a lot more polished. Its aluminium suspension uses longer arms to enable the extra-wheel travel you need on a car with off-road aspirations. It rides on nicely calibrated height-adjustable air springs and features chassis enhancements such as electronic dampers, torque vectoring and a limited-slip rear differential. Most of the power is sent to the rear axle most of the time, in time-honoured sports car fashion, until the car's systems detect otherwise, or you've actually ventured off-road, though God knows why anyone would ever do that.

Low-revving, smelly diesel is another concept that should be anathema to Maserati, but it's the power source that most SUVs use, so the Levante arrives in the UK armed only with a 3.0-litre turbo diesel. Actually, it's pretty good – torque enough to hustle 2.1 tonnes of Italian metal down the road with imperious ease, without sounding like a rattly, old freight train shunting up a Milanese railway siding.

The Levante needs 20in wheels to fill out its enormous wheel arches properly, but these don't punish the ride quality too badly. Nor does it loll or roll around as much as you'd expect given its increased centre of gravity. Maserati has stuck with hydraulic power steering (rather than the increasingly fashionable fully electric setup), so it's way more communicative than you might expect. In fact, in the quest to deliver the Maserati of SUVs, Maserati may just have served up the most 'Maserati' Maserati of the marque's current line up.

Especially if you tick the Zegna box and apply the same sartorial rules when it comes to configuring the Levante's handsome interior as you would at your tailor's. The appealingly louche undercurrent that the best Maseratis possess gets a new lease of life in the Levante, and what Italians refer to as *sprezzatura* gives it an edge over some of its more uptight rivals. Only this time it has the ability to go with the big personality.

Jaguar F-Pace
The special one

The Jaguar F-Pace is a true crossover champion. GQ joined another ice-cold icon – José Mourinho – in Sweden to talk torque, power sliding and keeping control in testing conditions.

GQ is in Arjeplog, a one-horse town in the far north of Sweden, where the horses swell in number every winter when the car industry decamps to inflict a brutal cold-weather testing regimen on still-secret new models. The last time we were here, the temperature plunged to a bracing -27°C (-17°F); today it's a positively balmy -4°C (25°F).

Jaguar is signing off its new 'crossover' the F-Pace, and José Mourinho is here to try it. If he's trying to escape the intense scrutiny that attends his every utterance, the edge of the Arctic Circle is a good place to do it. The former Chelsea, Real Madrid and Manchester United manager has always guided his teams to glory, even if sometimes the journey ended in tears. Hopefully that won't happen today, because this afternoon José is part of another team – the Jaguar team – and a Finnish ex-rally driver called Tommi is the coach that really matters. Jag's frozen test process doesn't begin until the ice is 50cm (20in) thick, and most of the work is gruellingly repetitive and necessarily empirical. But it's also fun: there's a lake nearby that's roughly the size of London and a chunk of it has been sequestered for test duty. *GQ* immediately finds itself power-sliding the F-Pace at wild angles and serious speeds, wondering how the hell a vehicle with a higher-than-usual centre of gravity can feel so alert.

There are various reasons for this. First, although Jaguar needs to enter this territory to meet its ambitious profit targets, no one wants a lumbering, dead-eyed behemoth. So the F-Pace is blessed with the same aluminium chassis as the XE and XF saloons, making it the only crossover so equipped (although its front suspension turrets have been reworked for extra ground clearance and the front cross-members have been enlarged).

Strong as it is light, it delivers the sort of sports-car handling most SUVs could only fantasize about. Its all-wheel drive uses a control system called Intelligent Driveline Dynamics, which ensures rear-drive poise unless the conditions demand extra grip, at which point 50 per cent of the torque is sent through the front wheels. There's also an electronic chassis system, Adaptive Surface Response, which accurately meters out grip even when it's slippery. The F-Pace groans with so much engineering detail that it's impossible to list it all, but if you want geeky, how about bonded bushes on the tubular anti-roll bar? This technique reduces noise, but also makes it difficult for dirt to work its way in. This stuff matters on a 4x4.

ENGINE
2,995cc supercharged V6, 380bhp

PERFORMANCE
0–62mph in 5.5 secs; top speed 155mph

YEAR OF RELEASE
2016

PRICE ON RELEASE
£34,170 ($57,700)

Not that anyone is ever seriously going to scale an alp in an F-Pace, but you can order it on huge 22in alloys. The version we're driving features the same 3.0-litre, 380bhp supercharged V6 as the F-Type roadster and coupé. Jaguar's design team has sweated the details so intensely that it really does look like a jacked-up F-Type – the body sides are formed from a single piece of aluminium – and it has a similar dynamism. Inside, it has Jaguar's latest touchscreen infotainment system, and there's emphasis on connectivity. Not all of it works perfectly, though, and, as with the saloons, there's a sense that most of the budget went on the shiny hard bits underneath.

Watching Mourinho on the ice, it's fair to say that this is a man unprepared to relinquish control. For the uninitiated, getting a car sideways is a leap of faith. 'It responds very well to every situation. Great responses, very stable, great fun,' he says succinctly afterwards. 'l once hit a patch of ice in Milan, and didn't like the experience. I think I would deal with it better now.'

How does he cope with the pressure? 'Football is not pressure for me – it is a privilege. I cope because it's easy to cope with something you like very, very much. That is why I don't understand when players don't enjoy their professional life. This is the kind of job where you are very well paid, but, at the same time, you live the dreams you had as a kid. It's why I sometimes have conflicts with people who don't share the same philosophy. You are in a sport to compete, you want to win, you hate to lose, you win once, so you want to win twice...When you are tired you can go home and give up your place to someone else.'

Has he learned everything there is to learn in football? 'No! I always have to learn. Even in football, which is an area in which I feel I am an expert, I am never perfect and I will always learn. Sometimes in my work, and also in my private life, maybe people think I am not humble. But I am so humble and I am always ready to learn from people who know more than me.' Indeed. And Tommi is waiting.

Bentley Bentayga
The best of all possible worlds

The super-powered Bentayga SUV was the most hotly anticipated car on the planet and GQ had exclusive access ahead of its launch.

Bentley's 21st-century Volkswagen-assisted renaissance reaches lofty new heights with its first SUV: the Bentayga. The mission statement is unequivocal: this will be the most luxurious, the most exclusive, and the fastest SUV in the world. Just don't call it a lorry. In fact, it might not have been an SUV at all. 'The brief was to expand the business,' product director Peter Guest says, 'not necessarily to create an SUV. The Continental GT [the aristocratic coupé, launched in 2003] was a game-changer for Bentley. We were tasked with finding the next one.'

In all honesty, you could swap 'game-changer' for 'no-brainer'. The SUV, whichever market stratum you look at, has become the default choice of an entire generation, in defiance of climate change, downsizing and the rejection of the car altogether by millennials. Trend forecasters, as *GQ* has previously noted, predict a global market of 20 million SUVs by 2020, of which a mere 30,000 will be so premium they're practically off the scale. This is the territory Bentley plans to own, and it's going to have the jump on upcoming rivals Aston Martin, Lamborghini and Rolls-Royce. Bentley plans to sell just 5,000 Bentaygas per year, adhering to the golden rule of supplying slightly less than the market demands in order to keep the flames of desire properly stoked.

In reality, the Bentayga sits so far up the automotive hierarchy that it's not an 'either/or car'; rather, it'll join a stable of other expensive cars. It also has a towing capacity of 3.5 tonnes, so it can handle a trailer-load of Arab stallions or a boat. Although, as one Bentley client apparently noted, if you can afford a Bentayga, your boat will be much too big to tow.

It's also that rare thing: a completely new car from the ground up. This is the sort of challenge designers and engineers love, although that clean sheet of paper is about as daunting as the blinking cursor at the top of a newly opened Word file at the start of a Don DeLillo novel. Bentley's SUV odyssey also got off to something of a false start with 2012's EXP 9 F, a vehicle so spectacularly inelegant even Uday Hussein would have rejected it as a bit OTT.

The Bentayga is a vast improvement, and manages to import Bentley's principal values – design, materials, exclusivity and individuality – into new territory. In other words, it doesn't look like a Range Rover or Porsche Cayenne, the two current SUV kingpins newly threatened with deposition; it looks like a big, jacked-up Bentley. It has the bluff, stately nose, the 'power

ENGINE
6.0-litre twin-turbo W12, 600bhp

PERFORMANCE
0–62mph in 4 secs; top speed around 187mph

YEAR OF RELEASE
2015

PRICE ON RELEASE
£162,700 ($229,100)

line' along its flanks and engorged, propulsive rear haunches. Whatever else you might think, you just know it's going to make a serious statement pulling up outside the Burj Khalifa or Claridge's.

There's a big technology story here, too. The body is made of aluminium, the use of which has carved 100kg (220lb) out of the car's overall weight. Ninety engine control units are used in the Bentayga, twice as many as the Continental GT and an indication of its complexity, and the new W12 engine manages to produce 600bhp, 6,641b ft of torque, and still emit less than 300g/km of CO_2. It also combines direct and port injection, has twin-scroll turbochargers and, among other deprivations, has done 400 hours testing at full throttle and two 400-cycle deep thermal shock tests. Bentley's sadists also subjected the car's interior to the equivalent of six months of intense sunlight.

It will also handle in a way that should enable a moderately ballsy driver to depose the Porsche Cayenne Turbo's ridiculous sub-eight-minutes lap time round the Nürburgring. The Bentayga is underpinned by a new air suspension, with four ride-height levels, and a 48-volt architecture governs its body control via electrically controlled anti-roll bars. On-road, this keeps the car's mass in check, regardless of the surface or speed, and guarantees maximum rolling comfort. Off-road, it ensures jaw-dropping axle articulation and the sort of capability no Bentley has ever dreamed of. 'We've vaulted forward two generations in one go,' Guest says. Siberia, here we come.

Inside, the Bentayga is replete with all the material majesty one associates with a brand that stores its wood in a humidor for a fortnight and sources its leather from the same Scandinavian supplier because it doesn't believe in barbed wire (it nicks the hide, you see). It will not be a rampant techno-fest, though, at least not one that assaults your senses in a crassly obvious way. Usable but invisible – if new luxury equates to simplicity, the Bentayga is in the vanguard.

'We're trying to appeal to a very tiny, extraordinary group of people,' Guest says. 'What is a Bentley SUV? Is it luxury or performance? For us, it's both. But there's an additional requirement for usability, and luxury doesn't stop when the tarmac does. Utility is a strange word to use in this context, but the Bentayga is the true expression of a 21st-century GT.'

Rolls-Royce Cullinan
At last! Rolls-Royce goes upwardly mobile

The marque that knows more than most about all things Plutusian bought into the latest licence to print money: a new luxury SUV. We took it to the wealthiest mountain range on earth to see if it made the gradient.

A Rolls-Royce 4x4. How you respond to those words will dictate how you feel about the Cullinan. This is either an exciting development or the end of days, and the 'statement' design – unusually deep windows, 'Parthenon' grille and a gallant adherence to Rolls's boldly surfaced proportions – is another polarizing factor.

What's indisputable is the intimacy of the relationship Rolls-Royce enjoys with its patrons; if they build it, they will come. And now the world's ultra-high-net-worth individuals (by which we mean a minimum of £25 million/ $32 million in disposable readies) have a car that can drive not just over the field of dreams, but up and over the mountain on the other side, in almost unimaginable luxury.

Rolls-Royces have always been robustly engineered, but there's still a perverse pleasure in pointing the Spirit of Ecstasy off the beaten track, knowing that neither she nor the rest of the car is going to flinch. The location of a first drive is usually incidental, but Jackson Hole in Wyoming isn't just cowboy country, it's also the wealthiest corner of America per capita (Harrison Ford has a ranch hereabouts). It's also 6,000ft above sea level, so it strains your lungs until you're acclimatized. The Cullinan is less bothered: it's powered by a reworked version of the engine used by the Phantom limousine, making 563bhp and 627lb ft of torque from 1,600rpm (a more powerful hybridized version is coming).

While our test route, framed by the magnificent Teton mountain range, isn't particularly demanding, the Cullinan still elevates Rolls's ride and refinement to a whole new plain – literally, in this instance – smothering off-road ruts and rocks in the same way the Phantom pulverizes regular roads. Self-levelling air suspension, which has a bigger volume for miraculous bump absorption, is crucial to its deportment. Electronically controlled dampers crunch body and wheel acceleration data in milliseconds, aided by a camera system that reads the road ahead. An adventure mode, meanwhile, is accessed via the 'Everywhere' button, which jiggles the traction control and uses hill descent software to tackle rutted track, gravel, wet grass, mud or snow. Its wading depth is 540mm (21in), the deepest, claims Rolls, of any super-luxury SUV. The Cullinan also has four-wheel steering and a 48-volt anti-roll system.

ENGINE
6.75-litre twin-turbo V12, 563bhp

PERFORMANCE
0–62mph in 5.2 secs; top speed 155mph (limited)

YEAR OF RELEASE
2018

PRICE ON RELEASE
£250,000 ($325,000)

Its structure is a reworking of what Rolls dubs the 'architecture of luxury', a modular aluminium spaceframe, with castings in each corner and extrusions in between, reconfigured here in a form that sits higher and shorter than the Phantom's, with a split tailgate for the necessary versatility. The Cullinan lacks the crazy axle articulation you need for really committed off-roading and relies mainly on increased ground clearance and cleverly networked ones and zeros to get you to places that nothing as sybaritic as this has ever been before. This is an extreme manifestation of experiential luxury.

That high body means an equivalently higher centre of gravity, which hurts handling. But not by much, and if that's what does it for you, you're clearly in the wrong place.

The transmission is the same velvety, satellite-aided ZF eight-speed automatic used by every other Rolls. The Cullinan doesn't really like to be rushed but, again, that's missing the point. This is an environment that promotes the old adage about it being better to travel hopefully than to arrive. Pretty soon, you realize that rushing is a terribly recherché concept anyway.

It's majestic inside. Real metal pillars connect the centre console and fascia and there's water-resistant 'box grain' black leather on the dash-top, doors and even the back of the key. The instrument dials have beautiful analogue graphics, and the central multimedia display now gains a touchscreen. Rear passengers sit higher than those in front, either in lounge configuration or sumptuous individual chairs (what fits in the space between is up to you, your bank balance but most of all your imagination).

Behind the split rear tailgate, the back can be specified with a Recreation Module, a motorized drawer designed according to the owner's preferred pastime, or a Viewing Suite, which stores a pair of folding, leather-clad rear-facing seats and a cocktail table in a special cassette.

This is, in so many ways, a ludicrous car. But in an era when the SUV is about the only sure thing for an embattled industry, creating the ultimate luxury off-roader is an opportunity Rolls-Royce had no option but to take up. The Cullinan is as meticulously engineered as you'd expect and a sublime place to lose yourself. But it's curiously hard to love.

Chapter 7
Road Tripping

To really get the best out of a car (or a motorbike), sometimes you have to take it – and yourself – out of its comfort zone. And *GQ* has never been afraid of hitting the road in search of a challenge. This chapter is all about some of our most memorable trips down memory lane, left at the Eiffel Tower, straight on through Death Valley, and ending up pining for the fjords. Through all of these adventures, though, the cars were always the stars. We definitely needed the Bentley Continental GTC to cross half of the United States, from the Napa Valley to Aspen. And what would have been the point in re-creating one of the most iconic scenes from *The Italian Job* (1969) without a classic E-Type Jaguar? Those are the excuses we're sticking with...

Bentley Continental GTC &
Bentley Continental Flying Spur
Once upon a time across America

Beating the heat in Death Valley, bartering with state troopers and braving the locals – a 2,000-mile drive through the Big Country was no small matter. Here's how, with the help of Bentley, the Wild West was won.

BENTLEY CONTINENTAL GTC

ENGINE
5,998cc W12 twin-turbo, 552bhp

PERFORMANCE
0–62mph in 4.8 secs; top speed 195mph

YEAR OF RELEASE
2007

PRICE ON RELEASE
£130,500 ($189,990)

BENTLEY CONTINENTAL FLYING SPUR

ENGINE
5,998cc W12 twin-turbo, 600bhp

PERFORMANCE
0–62mph in 4.5 secs; top speed 200mph

YEAR OF RELEASE
2007

PRICE ON RELEASE
£133,000 ($169,990)

In March 1930, Woolf Barnato accepted a wager. The three-time Le Mans-winning gentleman racer, first-class cricketer and heir to his diamond-mining father's fortune bet £200 that his Bentley could travel from the south of France to London quicker than Le Train Bleu could reach Calais. As the train left Cannes station at 5.45 in the evening, 'Babe' – an ironic moniker given that Barnato had the physique of a well-fed heavyweight boxer – fired up his Le Mans-winning Speed Six and headed out of the Riviera. At 3.20 the following afternoon, having crossed the English Channel by ferry, the British 'Bentley Boy' arrived at the Conservative Club in fashionable St James's Street. Four minutes later, Le Train Bleu arrived in the French port.

Romantic, courageous, dangerous, death-defying but, most significantly, ultimately successful, Barnato's drive was an historic achievement that has come to symbolize the Bentley story. During its life the marque has been insulted (legendary car designer Ettore Bugatti described the cars as 'the world's fastest lorries'), celebrated (in his 1953 book *Casino Royale*, Ian Fleming had 007 behind the wheel of a supercharged 4.5-litre Bentley), and suffered repeatedly the slings and arrows of outrageous misfortune, but through it all it remained the embodiment of automotive Brit-cool.

And back in 2007, and after nearly 90 turbulent years, the Bentley brand had never looked better, with increased global sales and its most extensive model range ever. So what better way to celebrate Bentley's 21st-century success than a challenge that would have got the original Bentley Boys as excited as discovering a troupe of drunken Tiller Girls hitchhiking alongside the Brooklands race circuit?

Of course, being *GQ* we couldn't merely retrace Barnato's route. For a start, even the French don't like driving in France, and what we wanted was a proper 'Grand Tour' that would bring out the best in Bentley's Continental GTC and the Flying Spur.

So we kept it simple and headed for America, the ultimate driving frontier: 2,045 miles, five days and as many states, two cars, one name. It would be a long journey, but Bentley has travelled much, much further...

DAY 1 – The Easy Start
MEADOWOOD to MAMMOTH, CALIFORNIA

If you thought California's Napa Valley was about wine, golf and casual sex, you've obviously seen the movie *Sideways* (2004). You can do those things, but when you have a Bentley GT Convertible, you won't want to.

Based on 2003's 'baby Bentley' coupé, the GTC is as masculine as its older brother but better looking. It is a throwback to the Bentleys that roared onto roads in the Twenties. Back then, an engineer, Walter Owen Bentley, or WO, had a simple mission for his post-WWI motor business: 'To build a good car, a fast car, the best in class.'

To prove he had achieved his aim, he took his 3.0-litre Bentley to the Grand Prix of Endurance near Le Mans. A fourth-place finish was the motivation WO needed to up his game. Thanks to investment from Barnato, he made his cars heavier, more powerful and more reliable, culminating in four Le Mans victories from 1927 to 1930, and the advent of the Speed Six. Named on account of its 6.5-litre, six-cylinder engine, the Six established Bentley's name and, although only 182 were made, it became the car to own.

The GTC comes with a mere 6.0-litre engine but, with twice as many cylinders as the Six, it produces 552bhp. Unbelievably, the 2.5-tonne GTC outweighs the Six, but it can still hit 195mph (190mph with its top down).

Handling like a dream on the twisting highways out of the valley and the harsher rural roads towards Jackson, the four-wheel drive, bionic chassis and comfortable seats mean that in Yosemite National Park it is easy to appreciate the giant lakes, cliffs and sequoias as your rear end is gently massaged.

It is also tempting to take your eye off the instrument panel. And even easier to forget that state troopers are tetchy when it comes to speeding. And that they carry guns. Oops. 'Good evening, sir...licence and registration.' Luckily, he lets us off with a warning under the proviso we give him a mention in *GQ*. But we have integrity. So we're very sorry, Officer Lawrence Kappel, a charming and well-dressed law enforcer from Mammoth, happily married to Darlene: no dice.

DAY 2 – The Fight for Survival
MAMMOTH, CALIFORNIA to LAS VEGAS, NEVADA

Sierra Nevada means 'snowy range' in Spanish. In September there isn't much of the white stuff, but it is cold. However, with the three-layered roof up you don't notice the biting mountain air. As soft tops go, the Continental's is a stunning piece of engineering. Steel bows are manoeuvred by a cantilevered folding mechanism that is so large it forced Bentley to redesign the rear suspension. And because it's a Bentley, you get a fabric roof that looks just right.

Inside, the Continental feels like the kind of place Winston Churchill might have dreamed of smoking cigars in. There is leather, polished veneers and steel knobs. The understated refinement evokes the days when Rolls-Royce took over Bentley Motors after the Great Depression. The partnership kept the marque alive, but at a price: over the years, Bentley merged into the Roller production line and lost some of its own identity.

Despite this union inspiring the first Continental after WWII, for purists it was the end of an era. However, although Bentley walked through the valley of the shadow of death, the name survived. And as *GQ* powers onwards to the 50°C (120°F) heat of Death Valley, we are thankful. The hottest place in America is barren, with more creepy-crawlies than a Bear Grylls packed lunch, yet the GTC doesn't flinch – unlike your reporter, who puts the roof up to embrace the air-con bosom.

On the other side of Death Valley is Nevada, and Las Vegas – 'the only town whose skyline is made up neither of buildings, like New York, nor of trees, like Wilbraham, Massachusetts, but signs', as Tom Wolfe said. Cruising the Strip, in the glow of its neon glamour, should be a Sinatra-inspired moment. The reality...'Hey buddy!'...is very...'Yo, buddy in the car!'...different. 'Sweet ride, dude! Can we get a ride up?'...The whirr of the roof ends one similar 'conversation' and any misconceptions about this Blackpool in the desert.

Ol' Blue Eyes would have wept...

DAY 3 – Striking It Lucky
LAS VEGAS, NEVADA to SEDONA, ARIZONA

Leaving Las Vegas wouldn't really be a hardship even if we didn't have the incentive of switching to a Flying Spur. Essentially the saloon version of the Continental, the Flying Spur is capable of 200mph and that makes it the fastest four-door car in the world. This statistic alone would put a smile on the faces of Bentley fans. Back in 1980, it only took one word to do that: Mulsanne.

When Rolls-Royce announced that it was naming a Bentley after the corner at the end of the longest straight at Le Mans, it was the first time since it had taken over the marque that Rolls had acknowledged Bentley's racing heritage. Suddenly, Bentley was alive again and the public welcomed the return in showrooms all over the country. A decade on from the Mulsanne, Bentley was outselling Rolls-Royce by two cars to one.

In engineering terms, Bentley's achievement was impressive...but only in relative terms. High above the Colorado River between Nevada and Arizona is the Hoover Dam, considered one of the seven wonders of the industrial world. It is a mesmerizing mix of magnificent Gothic architecture, mind-blowing natural beauty and a monument to mankind's ability to achieve the seemingly impossible (in less time than it took for 21st-century craftsmen to rebuild Wembley Stadium). Unfortunately, most of America is keen to take a look, so taking pictures on the Dam is pretty difficult because the state troopers insist on keeping the traffic moving. I mentioned they carried guns, right?

Driving into Arizona and onto the mythical 'Mother Road', Route 66, it's clear that most of the Main Street of America has now been abandoned in favour of the monstrous freeways, but it's worth seeking it out if you have the time. In fact, if you really aren't in a rush, you should stop off at Angel Delgadillo's barber shop just west of Flagstaff. Angel has been in residence there for decades and he seems to have spent most of that time deep in monologue.

But he knows a thing or two about cars, does Angel, and he knows what he likes. And he likes the Flying Spur. He wouldn't drive one, though. 'Hell no!' he says, genuinely appalled at the suggestion. 'Cadillac Eldorado Brougham, 1959, all the way, baby. Let me tell you about the Brougham....It's dark by the time we get to Sedona. And our ears ache.

DAY 4 – Reaching New Heights
SEDONA, ARIZONA to MOAB, UTAH

The sun blisters off the red rock as we head for what we have been assured will be the highlight of the trip: the Grand Canyon and Monument Valley. However, as far as geological phenomena go, they will have to go some way to beat the outcrop just outside Sedona that looks like Snoopy lying on his kennel. But the Grand Canyon doesn't disappoint. At 277 miles long and 18 miles wide, you could marvel at the vastness of this intricate landscape for hours...but that would mean getting out of the Flying Spur. And we've just bought an iPod connector. So we take pictures and continue our adventure.

Back in 1998, Volkswagen bid for Bentley. Sceptics assumed VW wouldn't give it the love it deserved, but they were proved wrong: with a huge investment and by the announcement that Bentley would be re-entering the motor-racing arena.

Five years later, Bentley scored a double achievement: it unveiled the Continental GT and, even more impressively, the Speed Eight finished first and second at Le Mans. Meanwhile, back in Monument Valley, we have also achieved a notable double. First, we don't get murdered in the shadow of the Mexican Hat (a rock formation so-called because it looks like...oh, you can guess). With a population of apparently just 50, when we take pictures we attract the attention of the more genetically disappointing members of the community. And second, we get the Flying Spur up to 165mph – the car does it with such ease, it would be easy to go faster but for the crying of the photographer. You do feel safe in the Bentley, though. Even when you are travelling at the speed of sound, it is such a solid and smooth drive that it feels as if you are travelling in an agile tank.

So with 'Dueling Banjos' playing, we wave goodbye to Monument Valley and the cast of *Deliverance* (1972), and hit the highway towards Moab.

DAY 5 – Back on the A-list
MOAB, UTAH to ASPEN, COLORADO

If Utah is all about vast Wild West scrubland and huge canyons, Colorado is much more mountainous and rural. If you look closely, you'll find wineries and viticultural areas aplenty, but in the Grand Mesa National Forest we find a long winding road that is an ecological marvel. At the base of the climb the climate is dry and arid. As we ascend along the curved black top the temperature falls, creating a cool mountain air in which Gambel oaks and pines thrive, until towards the summit the Grand Mesa becomes lush, wet and sub-alpine.

It is an eco-splosion of flora and fauna so dazzling you expect Al Gore to be at the top running an electric-car charging station. And we are driving a Flying Spur. In environmental terms, that's like turning up at a Greenpeace party in a suit of panda fur and riding a bike made from rhino horns. Especially as we keep doubling back for another photo opportunity. But if Bentley's carbon skid mark is the only potential speed bump it has to negotiate in 2007, it hasn't got too much to worry about.

In fact, as we charge along Route 92 towards Aspen, I can't help but think that both the Continental GTC and the Flying Spur may be two of the best cars I have ever driven. After five days of careful, mind-blowing, grand touring consideration, I really can't think of much to find fault with.

And as we arrive in Aspen, the picture postcard A-list resort, it is clear that I am not the only one enamoured of the marque. In a town where even the postmen drive Range Rovers and the hobos dress in Gucci, the Flying Spur is still attracting admiring glances. As we pull up outside the Little Nell hotel on Durant Avenue, where we are to hand back the keys, it is hard to believe that this trip is over. Of course, there is no point being a baby about these things.

'I'll be glad to see the back of this car,' I say to the photographer.
'Yeah, me too,' he replies. 'Good riddance to it…Then again, I might just try and get a few more interior shots. Just to be on the safe side.'
'Good idea,' I say. 'Just to be on the safe side, I'll come with you. I bet we could get great pictures in Chicago…'

Jaguar E-Type & XKR
On days like these

Hang on, lads, we've got a great idea... Jason Barlow and Celia Walden were partners in crime as GQ *took Jaguar's classic E-Type and the new XKR on an Italian job through the Aosta Valley.*

When you've got *Sinatra at the Sands* and the biggest album of all time – *Thriller* – on your CV, it's possible that the soundtrack to a camp little Sixties Brit flick might just have slipped to the back of your mind. Because when I brandished my soundtrack of *The Italian Job* in front of the chap who composed it, the incomparable Quincy Jones intoned: 'Man, I didn't think they'd even put that out on CD (...*long pause*). Let me tell you, Michael and I had some fun when I came to London to work on that film...'

Quincy Jones and Michael Caine, carousing together in London, in 1969? Fun, you suspect, would most definitely have been had. Technicolor fun the sort mere mortals can only dream of. As for *The Italian Job* itself, well even with one's irony filter firmly switched off, it remains a largely irresistible caper and still epitomizes a caddish sub-brand of cinema that's thoroughly and amusingly out of time 50 years later. With its fruity stereotypes, casual sexism and cartoon criminality, it's really just a lavishly appointed, more smoothly upholstered *Carry On* film. On the other hand, you can't argue with anything that has both Benny Hill and Noel Coward in it. Not to mention Quincy's gorgeous soundtrack, which, daft terrace anthem 'Self-Preservation Society' aside, is basically a jazz score.

And then there are the cars.

The opening credit sequence stars a Lamborghini Miura that still looks impossibly glamorous today. There are sexy Alfa Romeos, cute Fiats and, most of all, of course, there's a trio of apparently indestructible Minis (until they're plunged over a cliff, anyway). Plucky Brits to this day drive theirs to the Italian Alps to pay homage to a film that granted Britain's most famous mobile export cinematic immortality (even if BMC's PR visionaries couldn't quite see the point and insisted on selling the producers the cars, the fools).

For our own tribute, however, *GQ* has opted for something a bit more upscale. Which is why you find us roughly 2,600m (8,530ft) above sea level in the Colle del Nivolet with the latest Jaguar XKR convertible and its legendary predecessor – and another star of the film – the E-Type. Needless to say, we don't have the slightest intention of blowing the bloody doors, or any other important body part, off this delightful pairing.

JAGUAR E-TYPE

ENGINE
4,235cc, 265 bhp
PERFORMANCE
0–62mph in 7.4 secs;
top speed 149mph
YEAR OF RELEASE
1961
PRICE ON RELEASE
£2,097 ($5,695)

JAGUAR XKR

ENGINE
5.0-litre V8 supercharged,
510 bhp
PERFORMANCE
0–62mph in 4.6 secs;
top speed 155mph
YEAR OF RELEASE
2011
PRICE ON RELEASE
£83,900 ($102,000)

While the Beatles were still honing their skills, the E-Type is one of the things that first got the Sixties a-swinging. Yes, that's right, a car. Nearly 60 years ago, the E-Type made its debut at the Geneva Motor Show, instantly teleporting the car industry into a decade that would swiftly slip its austere post-war moorings and start partying. If you were lucky, you got to drive an E-Type to that party, although it's worth noting that it was much cheaper and therefore more accessible than any contemporary Aston Martin or Ferrari.

The E-Type's designer, Malcolm Sayer, insisted that the car was drawn according to strict mathematical principles, which may well be true, but doesn't alter the fact that this remains arguably the most overtly sexual-looking automobile ever made. Ferrari's 250 GTO offers a similar conflation of masculine thrustiness and sublime female sensuality, but it only made 36 of those and they cost rather more, then and now.

The Jaguar cost £2,097 15s ($5,695 – £38,000/$59,000 in today's money), and promised a top speed that was double the British speed limit. Not that you had to worry about a trifling little thing like a speed limit in 1961.

Like all old cars, get into an E-Type today and everything around you – doors, windscreen, pretty much all the handles, levers and buttons – seem to have been purpose-built to eviscerate the occupants in the event of an accident. It's also much smaller than you'd imagine; the top of my head peeps above the header rail of this roadster version, my legs are unattractively splayed and my knees brush against the steering column. Driving one of these at any sort of speed certainly concentrates the mind.

But what an experience it is. It helps that we're in the Aosta Valley and the sun is splitting the trees in great beaming shards. The original E-Type was powered by a 3.8-litre engine, but from 1964 the sonorous 4.2-litre, 265bhp, straight-six was available – it's a pretty vigorous performer even by today's standards. Push the weighty throttle pedal and you can physically sense the triple carburettors introducing fuel to air on its way to the intake valves: no fancy electronics here. The wood-rimmed steering wheel is similarly so large that my right elbow has nowhere to go but the top of the door, in the time-honoured grand-touring way. There's just no getting away from it: old cars simply have more charisma than their modern equivalents, and an E-Type is about as charismatic as it gets.

FASTER, PUSSYCAT

Alpine passes, impossible bends and Jaguar's super-stylish, 5.0-litre modern-day marque just begged to be pushed to its limits. Celia Walden rescinded her membership of the Self-Preservation Society...

'So this is it,' I think to myself. 'This is how I'm going to die.' It's a curiously unemotional thought – without any of the panic or sadness you'd expect to accompany the knowledge that you're minutes away from the End. Maybe that's because, all things considered, this isn't such a bad way to go. I'm driving a Jaguar XKR convertible at 110mph up a mountain in the Aosta Valley, there's an inordinately attractive 19-year-old boy in the passenger seat and I've just had one of those Italian croissants – the kind you forget are filled with custard until your tongue bursts the little pastry parcel in the middle and creamy sweetness is unleashed into your mouth. 'Faster,' mouths Alberto beside me, and I slam my foot down on the pedal.

You'd think I'd know by now that nothing good ever comes from the phrase, the editor's had an idea. 'He wants you to drive down to the Colle del Nivolet and re-create the car chase in *The Italian Job*,' came the explanation. And, for once, I was as enthusiastic as he was. All I was being asked to do was drive one of the most beautiful cars in existence across northern Italy alongside the aforementioned preternaturally good-looking Italian intern from Jaguar.

But here's the problem: while I'm a girl-racer back home, Italian roads (ever since a childhood incident involving a scooter and a one-way street in Rome) have always suggested 'instant death' to me. 'Blowing the bloody doors off' may not have been the plan, but in this car, with an E-type in front and those perfectly formed, lightly downed adolescent lips mouthing 'faster' beside me, I seem to have taken leave of my senses.

The XKR has a tendency to make you want to lose control. Driving one at 30mph around central London is like listening to the Pointer Sisters' 'I'm So Excited' while wearing a straitjacket. With its shapely, lightweight aluminium body and supercharged 5.0-litre V8 engine (which covers 0–62mph in 4.6 seconds and boasts a top speed of 155mph), this car is made to chase and be chased in.

I'll admit to a pang of jealousy when compared to the E-Type. But if you're navigating hillside hairpin bends with nothing between you and the hundred-foot drop on the right-hand side, you want the XKR's reliability and lightness of touch. That finely tuned suspension system and six-speed gearbox – with its behind-the-wheel paddles – can be trusted to keep the drive smooth, despite my ultra-quick gearshifts. Push the car to the kind of speeds I'm being coerced into driving and you can feel the suspension actively stiffen beneath you as it prepares to minimize body-roll.

So whereas that E-Type is going up and down like a sex-starved cheerleader in front, I can scarcely feel even the biggest lumps and bumps in the road. Try to slow down or brake, however, and the car seems more reluctant than the E-Type to do so. Whereas cruising is the older model's default position, too fast is what comes naturally to the XKR.

There's something else. If I'm going to die, I want to die in comfort, and my would-be luxury coffin (at 4,794mm/16ft long, the XKR is 200mm (8in) longer than the Mercedes SL and noticeably broader) is as roomy as a Saudi Arabian hotel suite. Inside the car, it's even plusher than the Mercedes' swanky inner cabin. With its thickly upholstered seats and uncluttered, matt-finished wood console, this car has one of the most elegant interiors I've ever seen.

As cosy as the XKR's confines are, you'd be foolish not to lower the hood the second you climb in – if only to relish that V8 exhaust note. It's the semi-active Ferrari-style system that gives the car its gravelly timbre under hard acceleration and I can't get enough of that distinctive sound. Growling, I catch up with the E-Type and we pass, inches apart, with the arches of the Pont d'Aël aqueduct within view. I can feel the road eating through my rear tyres, smell the clove-like scent of burning rubber and hear my Italian wingman...'Hang on a minute,' he chuckles, 'I've got a great idea!'

And for us, at least, I'm pretty sure the credits are about to roll...

Rolls-Royce Phantom Drophead Coupé
Rock et roller

GQ took a tour de France to test-drive that grandest of touring cars: the Rolls-Royce Phantom.

ENGINE
6,749cc V12, 453bhp
PERFORMANCE
0–62mph in 5.6 secs; top
speed 155mph (limited)
YEAR OF RELEASE
2008
PRICE ON RELEASE
£296,500 ($412,000)

When Jeremy Clarkson drove the Rolls-Royce Phantom Coupé, he reckoned he could not only feel the hate from every other motorist and pedestrian who spotted him on the road, but that he could actually see it and even smell it. The thing is, it is a very British view point. While our seething, credit-crunched underclass (and the environ-mentalists, of course) regard a car that costs twice as much as the average house with a vitriol usually reserved for Brexit negotiations, our European cousins just 21 miles across the Channel are far more laissez faire about it. Surprising really, when you consider that the French have a history of responding to displays of ostentation by firing up the torches and separating the fancy carriage-owner from not only his ride but also his head. Fortunately for *GQ*, times have changed in France and the former aristo-slaughterers now welcome English visitors in big 6.75-litre dreadnoughts with even bigger smiles and arms as wide as the Spirit of Ecstasy herself. And not just at petrol stations, either.

From the rural villages in northwestern France, down through the lush vineyards of the southwest to the Côte d'Azur, the Phantom Coupé is welcomed with a mixture of stunned surprise and welcoming waves. No sneering, no single-finger salutes and not even any comments about the possible shortcomings in my pantaloons. Instead, the jet-black behemoth marches through France in unopposed glory. And from the comfort of the driver's leather armchair, it is even more glorious.

Let's start with the sound: there isn't any. Even when you are effortlessly 'testing' the self-imposed electronic speed restriction of 155mph on *les autoroutes*, the most you get through the double-glazed windows is a gentle hum – like a vacuum cleaner sucking on the finest Axminster two rooms away. And that's very worrying. Not because you want to hear what that V12 can do, but because the gendarmerie apparently have the power to confiscate your vehicle if you are caught speeding. Luckily, what they don't lack in police powers, they more than make up for by having virtually no speed cameras. So you have to be pretty unlucky, or Lewis Hamilton (who lost the right to drive on French roads – not racetracks – after getting clocked doing a miserly 122mph), to get caught overdoing things here. Thank God. The truth, though, is that the point of a Rolls-Royce is not to drive it flat out.

It is a grand tourer in the grandest sense. From the largest N roads to the smallest streets of Monte Carlo, the Phantom navigates them all with a wonderfully graceful quality. There is an 'S for Sport' button you can press if you are feeling adventurous, but it would be a little gauche to do something like that. For a big car it's in great shape and, although it has the dimensions of a small barge (albeit a sporty one), it is as agile as a Chinese gymnast.

Which brings us neatly to the shortcomings of the Phantom Coupé: namely, just how few Chinese gymnasts you could actually fit in the boot or on the back seat. Not that we are condoning people-trafficking in a Rolls, of course, but if you did, you'd certainly expect to get more than half a dozen in there to make it financially viable.

In the traditional Rollers of yore, you'd have accommodated that number in the front ashtray. Elsewhere, the interior is predictably – and comfortingly – stately. The buttons and knobs feel like titanium paperweights, the wood panelling and leather seats are traditional, but in the style of a modern gentlemen's club, and the carpet is so thick you could lose a small dog in its fibres. The suicide doors – which you can close at the touch of a button – are heavy-metal 'thunkery' at its reassuring best. And the stereo, if you can get it to work with the embarrassingly lousy iPod connector, is better than the sound system at the O2 Arena.

But the real sound of the Rolls-Royce Phantom is hushed respect. From one end of France to the other, this British institution has been welcomed, photographed and fawned over. But after marching more than 2,000 miles through France, we are left with one unavoidable question: why are the French so humble before this car, while the British are so hateful? It is not until we bomb into Paris with cameras flashing and people cheering, that the answer becomes clear – at least to us. Rolls-Royce may represent Britain at its best, but it is now owned by the Bavarian Motor Works, aka BMW, aka the Germans. Which explains why we have been able to drive through France with barely an interruption, and why the British regard Rolls-Royces with barely concealed hostility. Sounds far-fetched, I know, but I have definitive proof. On the homeward drive back up from St Tropez to Paris, we spent the night across the Swiss border in Geneva, where no one seemed to have any opinion on the Phantom. They didn't love it, they didn't hate it...everyone seemed entirely indifferent. Even the hotel's valet-parking guy just smiled obligingly when I asked him what he thought of the car. Then again, that's the Swiss for you... still neutral after all these years.

Mercedes-AMG GT S
Where the wild things are

Following the fire-breathing SLS was always going to be a monster task for Mercedes-AMG. But, as GQ *discovered deep in the Norwegian fjords, they triumphed with the GT S – a gentle giant with the strength to move mountains.*

ENGINE
4.0-litre V8, 503bhp
PERFORMANCE
0–62mph in 3.8 secs;
top speed 193mph
YEAR OF RELEASE
2015
PRICE ON RELEASE
£110,500 ($130,825)

Fans of Monty Python will know all about the Norwegian Blue. However, for the benefit of millennial petrolheads, allow me to explain. This cult comedy sketch sees John Cleese complaining to pet-shop spiv Michael Palin that he has been sold a dead parrot. After much hilarious toing and froing (sorry, I can't do the voices), Palin explains that the remarkable bird – with its beautiful plumage – hasn't actually 'kicked the bucket, shuffled off his mortal coil, run down the curtain and joined the bleedin' choir invisible', as Cleese claimed. The reason for the Norwegian Blue's apparent lack of life is down to one thing: he is pining for the fjords.

Now, some 50 years after that surreal routine was first broadcast, I finally get the joke. And having spent three days driving around the most incredible strips of tarmac in Norway, I can tell you it really isn't funny (despite all the *Radio Times* accolades). Pining for the fjords is a very real and truly terrible affliction. As is pining for the Mercedes-AMG GT S.

Introduced by the Stuttgart-based carmaker in 2014 as the successor to (not a replacement for, Mercedes pointed out) the bombastic and bonkers gull-winged SLS, the GT was conceived as a smaller, stripped-back sports car that would cost less than its big brother, deliver more driver excitement and be a full-on, full-fat, muscle-car rival to the Porsche 911 Turbo, the Jaguar F-Type and the Audi R8. In other words, Mercedes-AMG set themselves a pretty high bar...but they have cleared it with Olympian ease.

Developed entirely in-house, what the GT S lacks in brute force (the SLS packed a 6.3-litre supercar punch that delivered a 199mph top speed) it makes up for in on-road refinement, sleeker and sexier styling and, dare we say, practicality. Because to be a genuine GT, this car not only has to look the part, make the right noises (Metallica couldn't generate this much stereophonic thunder) and handle like a Grand Theft Auto cheat code, it also needs to be usable. That means: all-day motoring comfort (tick). Desirable driving position (tick). Boot space (tick). And even back seats (tick, if you are travelling with Warwick Davis).

The GT S would, quite simply, look good anywhere. But to get the most out of it, you need to really be somewhere, and few places on earth have roads that can compete with Norway's.

From the snow-capped peaks and the stunning switchbacks of the Trollstigen Mountain Road (aka Troll's Ladder), through to the spectacular curved bridges of the coastal Atlantic Road, if ever there was a country worthy of automotive exploration, it is this one. *GQ*'s advice would be to aim for late May/early June, when all of the roads have reopened after winter and daylight stretches out for close to 20 hours.

That's the good news. The bad news is that although there aren't a great number of safety enforcement cameras in the country, speeding and general traffic offences are subject to extremely heavy on-the-spot fines.

The other danger with driving in Norway is that the weather conditions can be hazardously unpredictable. Driving rain, blizzards and snowstorms can hit at any time. Freezing fog and ice can make the roads treacherous. Even in a car as well balanced and as grippy as the Mercedes-AMG GT S, if you lose concentration, you'll soon discover that all the Collision Prevention Assists, driver and passenger knee airbags and blind-spot warnings in the world won't stop you from plummeting hundreds of feet down rocky outcrops.

But don't let something like plunging into an icy fjord in a ball of flames discourage you from exploring this incredible country. You might end up as dead as the Norwegian Blue, but it really would be a hell of a way to go...

Harley-Davidson Breakout
Find riding heaven on the highway from hell

'Ceaușescu's Folly' was built through the foothills of Romania to aid the dictator's flight from the country he ravaged, and was paved with the graves of his own people. Today, safe in the saddle of the Harley-Davidson Breakout, GQ staged an escape of its own on the world's greatest road.

What have the Romanians ever done for us? I mean, apart from inventing the fountain pen, being home to Dracula, having the world's largest underground salt-mine museum and, according to the political commentators at the *Daily Mail*, off-loading as many thieving, dead-eyed, gypsy pickpockets as their airports can handle, you'd be forgiven for thinking, not much. But spare a thought for the Romanians themselves.

Having only been a truly independent country since 1878, Romania's modern history has been a tale of hostile invasion (in WWI and WWII), fascist violence (the nationalistic and anti-Semitic Iron Guard), Soviet occupation (up to the late Fifties) and, probably worst of all, brutal communist dictatorship. Under the ferociously repressive 22-year reign of President Nicolae Ceaușescu, millions of Romanians were starved, terrorized, tortured and executed by a regime so brutal that it was compared to that of Stalinist Russia. When communism fell in 1989, the Romanian Revolution brought an end to Ceaușescu's rule and he and his wife, Elena, were tried and executed by firing squad on Christmas Day.

The damage the self-proclaimed *conducător* (leader) did to Romania can clearly still be felt today, especially when you explore the country beyond Bucharest. Drive north and, once you reach the countryside, you will notice many things that you wouldn't normally find in Europe. There are also a disproportionate number of HGVs, which probably explains why if you pass the right truck stop in the mid-afternoon sunshine, you will see teenage prostitutes cheerlessly keeping weary drivers on the straight and narrow. And who knew any nation still sold scythes in such vast quantities? Every village seemed to have a shell-suited Grim Reaper tending some woeful dusty crops, human misery etched on their swarthy face.

And yet despite these constant reminders of Ceaușescu's years of misrule, it is hard for non-Romanians to completely dismiss the man who called himself the *Geniul din Carpati* (the Genius of the Carpathians). And that is for one simple reason: he built what is possibly the greatest road in the world.

The Transfăgărăçan highway, aka DN7C, aka Ceaușescu's Folly, is just 60 miles long and was built by the old dictator as a response to the Soviet invasion of Czechoslovakia in 1968. If Romania was to be targeted next, the president reasoned, he wanted an escape route for himself (and his precious secret

ENGINE
1,690cc twin cam
PERFORMANCE
0–62mph in 4.7 secs; top speed 114mph
YEAR OF RELEASE
2013
PRICE ON RELEASE
£15,895 ($18,499)

police) across the Făgaraç Mountains. It required 6,000 tonnes of dynamite to carve out a path, took four years to build, and cost so many lives (estimates say as many as 100) that the official documentation of death was forbidden. It was an exercise in hubris from a man who refused to abandon the project, even though he was aware that even when the road was completed it would only be passable for around four months of the year.

Luckily for Ceauşescu, the Russians never felt that attacking Romania was worth the effort. Subsequently, however, the Transfăgărăçan Highway has attracted interest from two- and four-wheeled invaders from all over the world, keen to conquer one of the most remarkable and unforgettable stretches of tarmac ever built. Visit between July and October and you will see any number of high-powered cars and bikes with as many different national number plates. *GQ*, however, could think of no better vehicle on which to explore this communist-created king of carriageways than the ultimate symbol of capitalist freedom: a Harley-Davidson.

And not just any old Harley. The tyre-squealing hog best suited to this theme park for automobiles is the Breakout.

Inspired by the gasser drag bikes of the Sixties, at first glance this 21st-century Softail is all big wheels (at 240mm/9 ½in), the rear tyre is the widest in H-D production history), chopped fenders, a stretched body and a low profile. Add to that its flat handlebars, extended foot pegs and custom design, and the Breakout looks like a fully fledged quarter-mile killer. The gutsy 1,690cc V-twin does nothing to dispel this impression. And a crank of the right hand confirms it. Clad all in black and howling through Transylvania, nothing has inspired this much fear and ferociousness in the Carpathian Mountains since Vlad III, Prince of Wallachia, discovered the joys of impaling.

However, while it is all very well hitting the highway like a vampire bat out of hell, what happens if you aren't travelling in a straight line? If say, you were riding on a road with more curves, bends, bumps and hairpins than a yoga session at the Playboy Mansion. Let's put it this way, tilt any more than 23.4 degrees and you'll soon get used to the scraping sound of foot peg on black top. And that's a pity because the Breakout handles very well for a heavy Harley.

That might sound like a backhanded compliment, but it really isn't. On the day *GQ* rode the Transfăgărăçan, it was wet and misty, the road gravelly and greasy; there was no margin for errors, nor roadside barriers to make up for them. It takes a little getting used to and more than a little blind faith, but the Breakout is reliably rock-solid in every turn. It obviously suits the straights far better, but the Harley engineers deserve a lot of credit for this particular chassis, because despite spending a couple of days in the saddle, covering the better part of 500 miles, there was not a single groan of complaint from either my back or buttocks. In other words, it really does ride as good as it looks. (You wouldn't want company, however...the pillion perch wouldn't even suit a passenger of Peter Dinklage proportions.)

And that might be Harley's greatest achievement with this bike. By combining the classic heritage styling with modern mechanics, they may just find they can appeal to the old-school Knucklehead and Panhead purists, as well as the latest generation of state-of-the-art street-bike supporters. On this day, on this road, in these conditions, they have certainly convinced me. That's how good the Breakout is.

And how good is the Transfăgărăçan highway? Well, it might not be the very best road in the world, but it is definitely one of them. And don't just take our word for it. On a notable internet travel website, it is rated as the fourth best attraction in Transylvania. By comparison, the Turda Salt Mine museum is only eighth. As Nicolae Ceauşescu probably said many times to his downtrodden construction team in the early Seventies, one day you, *GQ* and TripAdvisor will thank me for this.

Chapter 8
The Millionaire's Club

Don't you just hate it when you pull into a parking space and there in the next bay is a car just like yours? Well, unless you live in Monaco, with the cars in this next chapter you probably won't have that problem. With a starting price somewhere north of seven figures and being produced in seriously limited-edition numbers, these automotive works of art aren't going to be popping up on eBay too often. These are the fastest, most ferocious, truly fantastic cars ever built, and we just had to take them for a spin. So if you have ever wondered what it's like to get behind the wheel of a Bugatti Chiron and not quite reach its 261mph top speed; drive flat out down the Virgin Galactic runway in New Mexico in an Aston Martin One-77; or experience a hot lap on the Fiorano test track in a Ferrari FXX...well, the next few pages are probably as close as you will ever get. Oh, and we threw in a speedboat just in case you had another million burning a hole in your pocket.

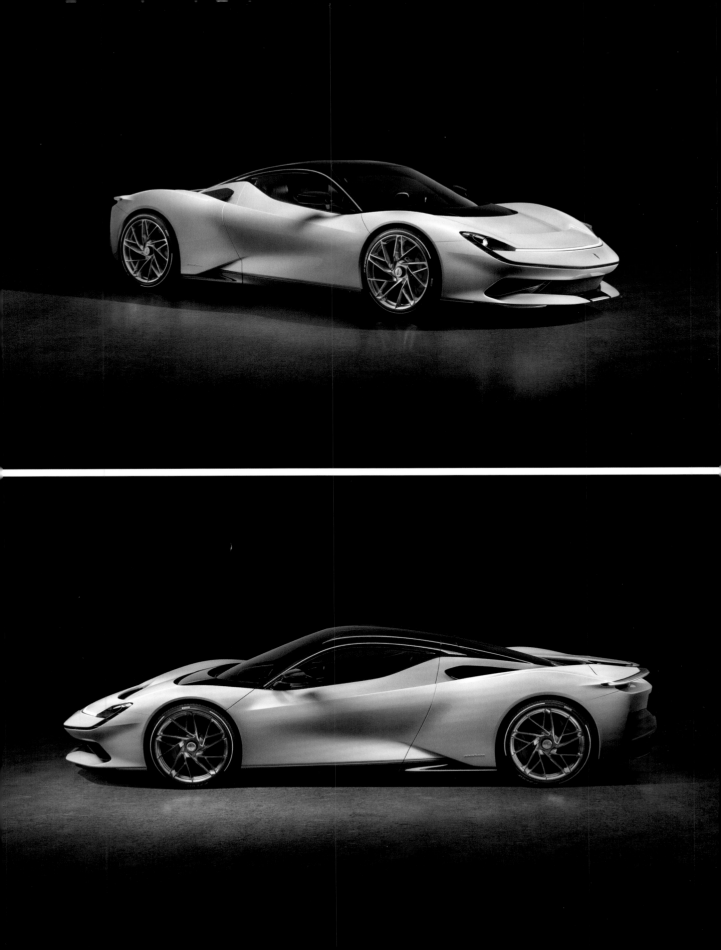

Pininfarina Battista
Italy's fastest-ever hypercar

The artiste coachbuilder that shaped countless Ferraris, Lancias and Maseratis flicked the switch on a car of its own: the all-electric, 1,900bhp Pininfarina Battista.

If you accept that automotive design is a legitimate art form – no question – then Battista 'Pinin' Farina has contributed more to this branch of human endeavour than anyone else. He is the lodestar, the Picasso or Warhol. Even New York's Museum of Modern Art had to acknowledge his influence. There aren't many cars in its permanent collection, but Farina's Cisitalia 202 is one of them, a deceptively simple-looking little coupé that set the entire automotive industry on a new aesthetic path when it appeared in 1947. And this at a time when Italy was still picking its way through the rubble of war, its factories decimated.

Cisitalia would be a footnote were it not for Farina's company, Carrozzeria Pininfarina, reimagining the body as a single volume, rather than a series of conjoined elements. Before World War II, other designers had been playing with this form, and early forays into air-cheatingly streamlined bodies pointed the way (including Pininfarina, in 1937, with the Lancia Aprilia Aerodinamica). But the 202 was something else, its aluminium panels hand-beaten over a wooden buck to set the template: perfect proportions, propulsive volumes to generate a sense of speed, minimal decoration.

Pininfarina went on to be fêted by kings and presidents, and from 1952 until very recently clothed almost every single Ferrari, among numerous other Alfa Romeos, Lancias and Maseratis. The company now has tendrils that have taken it into furniture, bridges, buildings, trains and aerospace. But, ironically, this great automotive couturier has never actually created a car of its own – until now. And the Pininfarina Battista is named in honour of the man who started it all.

A new company, Automobili Pininfarina, has been created in parallel with the Pininfarina SpA mothership, with a plan to sell a total of 150 Battistas at a cost of approximately £2 million ($2.58 million) each. It might look like a generic, though mesmerizingly beautiful, mid-engined hypercar, but it's pushing the form to the outer limits – not least because the Battista is purely electric and shuns the emotional but increasingly anachronistic internal combustion engine in favour of zero emissions and a superficially guilt-free ultra-performance.

Producing the equivalent of 1,900bhp, it can claim to be the most powerful Italian road car ever made. Zero to 62mph takes less than two seconds,

ENGINE
Four electric motors generating 1,417 kilowatts (1,900bhp)

PERFORMANCE
0–62mph in under 2 secs; top speed 250mph

YEAR OF RELEASE
Yet to be released

PRICE ON RELEASE
From £2 million ($2.58 million)

186mph is up in under 12, and the top speed is likely to be 250mph, with a projected range of 300 miles from the batteries, assuming you're not travelling at warp five everywhere. A superfast charging system will replenish the batteries to 80 per cent capacity in just 40 minutes.

The body is made of carbon fibre, with the batteries housed behind the occupants and along the sides in a T-format. The electrical architecture is being co-developed with another EV outfit, the Croatian firm Rimac (itself 10 per cent owned by Porsche and said to be consulting with numerous manufacturers on this fast-moving technology). As you'd hope, given the price and provenance, the interior is swathed in the finest materials, although as the product of what's billed as the world's first sustainable luxury car company, nontraditional techniques are being explored.

'Pininfarina's mission is to design cars that are innovative, pure, simple, elegant,' chairman and Battista's grandson, Paolo, tells me. 'This project was a great challenge because we are designing for ourselves here, so we want it to be Pininfarina 110 per cent. It's not a negotiation or a compromise: this is us. Why should you be attracted to a Pininfarina car? Because it's beautiful, it has harmony, it's innovative but has classic qualities. Electrification is the future.'

Ask him why Italy historically outranks every other country in car design terms and Paolo revs up an interesting theory.

'It's a matter of people. My grandfather, Battista, was an outlier, one in a million. To succeed as an outlier you need three things: talent, commitment and to be born at the right moment and in the right place. He was born in 1893, in Turin, surrounded by other talented people who were exploring the future of the car. With these things, success came.'

The story runs deeper, though, and it's ironic that Pininfarina's first own-brand car only exists because this Italian legend was sold to Indian behemoth Mahindra in 2015 for £147m ($220m). The company's executive chairman, Anand Mahindra – a Harvard graduate in film studies rather than a hard-boiled businessman – is enabling a plan that might well have continued to elude Pininfarina on its own.

'The [Battista] will enable us to fulfil our vision of participating at the pinnacle of automotive design,' he says. 'Luxury is the meeting point of heritage and craftsmanship, which is what Pininfarina has. It would take 90 years to build what Pininfarina has.'

The bigger picture here is as compelling as the car itself. Mahindra believes that car ownership will follow three paths during the next few decades: an autonomous, fully electric one in which simple utility is key; cars for recreational use; and 'cars that are bought purely because they are objects of desire, out of passion for performance and beauty'. In addition, Automobili Pininfarina will license the hardware from other companies to avoid crippling investment in proprietary technology – the asset-light business model of which Apple is the most profitable exponent. It's unlikely the Battista could exist otherwise.

That said, it's still channelling some old-fashioned magic, as chief designer Luca Borgogno says: 'This was the most important part of the first briefing: it has to be beautiful. Look at the cars in our museum: what really strikes you is the purity and beauty. *Purezza e bellezza*.'

Ferrari FXX
Special FXX

GQ joined driving's super-elite in the first Ferrari to cost seven figures.

ENGINE
6.2-litre V12, 800bhp
PERFORMANCE
0–62mph in 3.0 secs;
top speed 225mph
YEAR OF RELEASE
2005
PRICE ON RELEASE
£1 million ($1.9 million)

There's a man standing at the end of the pit lane at a secret racetrack, frantically waving a red flag. In the world of motor racing, this is the equivalent of a giant 'stop' sign. Keep going under a waved red and you'll get your backside kicked into next week by the authorities.

We keep going. Over the furious din of the 6.2-litre V12, I'd previously shouted to Luca Badoer, the Ferrari Formula One test driver, to 'hang back a bit, then give it some' up the pit straight. None of which translates well into Italian, but he seems to have the drift. Within seconds, red flag man is a distant speck, and the Ferrari is bearing down on the tight right with a thunderous enthusiasm that has squeezed the air out of my lungs. Will we make it? God knows. Nothing I have ever been in has ravaged its way around a circuit with such hunger. Gear changes are gone in imperceptible milliseconds, directional changes are almost telepathic, and the acceleration is genuinely eye-popping. On the automotive totem pole, surely only a Formula One car could top this?

And that's the point. This is the Ferrari FXX, arguably the most exclusive car on the planet, and Ferrari's inordinately special gift to its most valued customers. Though gift is hardly the word: only 29 will be made, two will end up in the UK, and for that privilege their new owners will each have paid £1 million ($1.9 million). Which, at the time of this car's release in 2005, makes it the world's most expensive new Ferrari.

The payback, should anybody with that much cash to spare on a car actually be bothered, is more than a bit special (more special than a Manhattan apartment, Caribbean island or new yacht, the likely items on the same stratospheric shopping list). All Ferrari customers are lucky, but some are luckier than others. With the FXX, you become part of the family, a 'client test driver', and actively involved in the development of the next generation of Ferrari road cars. Sure, you get the car, but you also get a bunch of track days, your own team of hand-picked technicians, the opportunity to constantly tweak the car to your own specification, and Italy's most famous man (and former Ferrari boss) Luca di Montezemolo will probably take a personal interest in how your kids are getting on at school. For a company as closely knit and guarded as Ferrari, it's a big deal. It's also something only Ferrari can do, a big money ticket into the richest, most celebrated car culture there's ever been.

At a time when Ferrari's road cars have become remarkably civilized, the FXX is hard-core. It's designed for track use only, and its body – an unpretty evolution of the wonderful Enzo – is a slave to the whims of aerodynamics. There are new wings, ducts and spoilers, wind-tunnel honed to cheat and manipulate air flow around the car. The engine's volume has increased to 6,262cc, its power output has shot up to 800bhp (from Enzo's 660bhp), and there's a new combustion chamber, crankcase, inlet and exhaust system. It has 40 per cent more downforce and weighs only 1,155kg (2,547lb). There are no mirrors; instead, a fin-shaped, roof-mounted camera shows what's going on behind on a dash-mounted screen. It's the only pointless gadgetry in a car that's otherwise built to do nothing except perform at the highest level (though you wouldn't want to prang it reversing into the garage).

It's also a rolling test bed. 'We'll use the FXX programme to define the parameters on our new supercar,' Ferrari vice-president Amedeo Felisa tells me. 'Right now, it is a showcase for the know-how that we have in our company. But the car also needs to be something our top customers can enjoy driving.'

No kidding. Badoer, who helps hone Ferrari's Formula One cars, looks more than happy. The FXX moves with grace and savage pace; since most of it is basically engine, it gathers momentum in a way that redraws the rat/drainpipe analogy. 'The tyres are cold,' Badoer says as he expertly collects the FXX's wayward rear on the entry to a corner, 'and even with this much downforce it's still not a Formula One car...' A pause. 'But the engine, well, the engine is not so far away.'

And with that, he shifts down two gears on the column-mounted paddles, smiles and squeezes the throttle pedal. Out of the corner of my eye I can see the man with the red flag smiling broadly. He's not the only one.

Aston Martin One-77
The space race

GQ touched down at the world's first commercial spaceport and took flight (well, nearly) in the Aston Martin One-77.

At the official opening of Spaceport America in the Jornada del Muerto desert in New Mexico in October 2011, Sir Richard Branson made his entrance in typically understated fashion by abseiling down the glass front of the Sir Norman Foster-designed building, before popping open a bottle of champagne and posing for the cameras with his biggest Virgin Galactic grin. And despite the then £125,000 ($200,000) ticket price, 460 space tourists from 46 countries had already paid for their flights in advance (including actress Victoria Principal, film director Bryan Singer, F1 driver Rubens Barrichello and comedian Russell Brand) and are currently forming an orderly queue ahead of the inaugural trip.

Unfortunately, being from *GQ*, being impatient and being an inveterate queue jumper, I just couldn't wait that long. Which is why, beneath a cloudless sky, I am sitting anxiously at the end of a long runway in a futuristic cockpit waiting for blast-off. The pilot, Chris Porritt, checks that I am securely strapped in, then, without so much as a countdown, we have blast-off. Pinned to my leather seat, the acceleration is as exciting as it is severe. In less than four seconds we are nudging 60mph, and the small crowd watching agape disappears in a blur.

Over the perfect storm of sound from the bawling engine, Porritt checks that I am OK. There is a grin on my face when I give him a thumbs-up affirmative, then we are pushed back into our seats again as our velocity pushes on into three digits. The ride is smooth, definitely comfortable, and from my vantage point I can see the numbers roll round: 130...140...150...160. 'Here we go,' says Porritt. 'Check this out.' And he takes his hands off the wheel and our course doesn't flicker an inch. At 170, back in control the acceleration begins to slow. 180: the pressure eases on my back. This is it. 190: any second now the nose will come up. 191: the final frontier. 192: ET, put the kettle on, I'm coming home. And at 193mph, it happens. Porritt slams on the ceramic brakes.

'That's the fastest we've done today,' he says calmly. 'If we'd been out earlier this morning, when the air was cooler, we'd have made it past 200mph easily.'

I wasn't actually allowed in the mothership (*WhiteKnightTwo*, AKA *VMS Eve*, named after Richard's mother), the detachable spaceship (*SpaceShipTwo*, AKA *VSS Enterprise*), or even within 20ft of Branson (he's a busy man). Instead, I was enjoying a passenger ride in the new Aston Martin One-77.

ENGINE
7,312cc, 48-valve V12, 750bhp
PERFORMANCE
0–62mph in 3.6 secs; top speed 220mph
YEAR OF RELEASE
2009
PRICE ON RELEASE
£1.2 million ($1.39 million)

This is an event, in automotive terms, almost as significant as the Spaceport opening. It is the first time anyone who doesn't have the wherewithal to bang down a deposit has been able to experience the One-77 on the road (OK, runway). Originally conceived as the ultimate demonstration of Aston Martin's design aesthetic and engineering capabilities, it took three years to travel from drawing board to production line. Then another year from unveiling to this point and passenger rides. On the basis of what I've just experienced, not only was it worth the wait, but it almost justifies its £1.2 million ($1.39 million) price tag.

Then again, when you consider that Virgin Galactic had at the time of writing spent £175 million ($229 million) on its space programme, and that construction of Spaceport America cost £132 million ($173 million), the One-77 seems like a snip. It certainly looked that way to one prospective buyer who was given a test run that morning. Having been behind the wheel, under the supervision of Aston's chief engineer, he emerged from the fun seat laughing excitedly and reaching for his chequebook. Aston is only making 77 of these machines, and they are down to the last seven (better make that six), so there is a market for a 7.3-litre, V12 hypercar. And they are going fast.

The One-77's statistics, however, are not quite as impressive as the Virgin Spaceship's. 'The climb up to 50,000ft in the mothership takes about 45 minutes and is just like a normal flight,' says Stephen Attenborough, Virgin Galactic's commercial director. 'But at that height, the spaceship with the six passengers and two pilots disengages and the hybrid rocket fires. Then the spaceship accelerates to 2,600mph, which is around 3.5 times the speed of sound. That's probably a little quicker than the Aston. And in just 90 seconds you'll be suborbital, flying to around 360,000ft [68 miles].'

Once the *VSS Enterprise* reaches that height, the rocket cuts out and the paying passengers get a few minutes of weightlessness, before the descent begins. Historically, getting back into the atmosphere has always been the hard part, but as this is a commercial vehicle, Virgin wants to be able to reuse the spaceship. 'What the designer, Burt Rutan, wanted was something that didn't rely on computers, didn't rely on pilots, but relied on nature,' explains Attenborough. 'So he came up with the shuttlecock idea.'

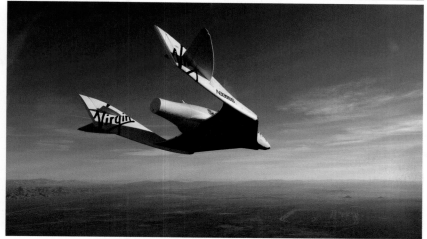

Rutan worked out that if he could change the shape of the craft out in space, when it starts to return to earth as gravity begins to take hold, it would fall the same way every time. 'The rear section rotates about 60 degrees to create a "feathered" re-entry position', explains Dave Mackay, Virgin Galactic's chief pilot. 'This slows descent, meaning there is no heat build-up, and pilots don't have to do anything until about 70,000ft when we press a button, the tail section returns to normal and the craft glides smoothly back to Spaceport America. The passengers get their astronaut wings and have a party.'

When you consider that, so far, only 525 people have actually been into space, this surely is reason enough to celebrate. Virgin's intention is to take 500 people up in the first year (Branson and his children Sam and Holly will be on the inaugural flight), but long-term projections are to fly into space on a daily basis. And, unsurprisingly, interest has been immense. As well as a number of celebrities, NASA has already block-booked some flights, and Virgin has also had enquiries from individuals who want to take all six seats for themselves, and perhaps one special friend. Attenborough does the maths quickly. 'I think that would qualify as the 68-mile high club.'

If an individual takes all the seats for themselves (and a guest), they get a small discount. Still, it would still be a lot to pay for a ride that will only last five minutes. Which brings us back to what a bargain the Aston Martin One-77 is.

After all, if you're travelling to infinity and beyond, you would certainly want to be dropped off in style.

Bugatti Chiron
Who puts the hyper in hypercar?

£2.5m ($3m) bought the fastest vehicle on the road, so why were Britain's slowest streets its favourite haunt? To find out, GQ *took the Bugatti Chiron on a head-turning tour of London's W1.*

ENGINE
8-litre, quad-turbo-charged W16, 1,479bhp
PERFORMANCE
0–62 mph in 2.5 secs; top speed 261mph
YEAR OF RELEASE
2016
PRICE ON RELEASE
£2.5 million ($3 million)

In the pioneering days of motoring, cars were such an infernal nuisance that legislators demanded a man walked ahead while waving a red flag. Such were the perils of an automobile that could do 10mph.

More than a century later, we're serenaded by the modern equivalent: the YouTuber brandishing a smartphone. Central London being one of the key global destinations for hypercars, the latest, the Bugatti Chiron, has been a mobile electromagnet for the past hour in Carnaby Street. It's a car of such vast shock value and presence that tourists have literally been falling over themselves to get a closer look. You can't blame them: chances are, they'll never see another one in their lifetime.

Now, as we ease the Chiron, all £2.5 million ($3 million) of it, into the gloopy, mid-morning traffic, plotting a course across Mayfair to The Dorchester hotel, we're followed the whole way by that peculiar breed of auto paparazzi that have staked out one corner of the internet. The Chiron's top speed might be 261mph – the limit of the tyres' capability, not the car itself – but right now it's doing one of the other things it's very good at: going as slowly as is dramatically possible. In an Instagram world, this is manna from heaven.

But it might also make the Chiron the world's most singularly pointless vehicle. Most cars are actually over-engineered and even the humblest airport rental has depths none of its users will ever locate. So ponder the lengths to which Bugatti has gone to make a car with 1,479bhp work in every market around the world that its parent company, Volkswagen, sells cars in, and one that delivers the endurance of a Golf in an Arctic blizzard or a desert in Dubai (more likely the latter). The Veyron, the Chiron's remarkable predecessor, was described as the automotive world's 'Concorde moment' by James May on an episode of *Top Gear*, but for various reasons – some emotional, others fiscally pragmatic – mankind stepped away from that supersonic achievement. Bugatti, though, has come back for more.

So what is it like? You get asked that a lot when people find out you've driven a Chiron and the answer is simple yet also surprisingly complicated. It's monumentally fast, of course, but so much more besides. The day before we rocked London, *GQ* had six hours in the countryside to acclimatize, in the company of Bugatti test driver Andy Wallace. Now retired, Wallace was a phenomenally accomplished racing driver, a winner at Le Mans in the famous

Silk Cut Jaguar XJR-9LM in 1988, who set a world record for the fastest production car a decade later in the McLaren F1 (240.14mph). Now he does customer handovers for Bugatti, a whole new hair-raising career dimension, for which his gentle but wry demeanour is well suited. 'It's a pity we're not on a runway today,' he tells me. 'The Chiron really comes alive above 150mph.'

This is a car that needs a runway. It only gets into its stride when most other cars are done. Even so, anything that can accelerate to 62mph in 2.5 seconds, 124mph in 6.5 and 186mph in under 13.6 is perfectly capable of rearranging vital internal organs on a normal road. That's a standard part of the road tester's lexicon, but the Chiron moves so quickly that strange sensations genuinely do occur in the pit of your stomach. It's mostly pleasant, although the rapidity with which traffic up ahead arrives in the windscreen is terrifying to begin with.

The experience is dominated by its engine. In the Chiron, you're always aware that something vast and otherworldly is doing unholy things to fuel and air right behind your head. It's 8 litres in capacity and features 16 cylinders and 4 turbochargers, like the Veyron, but uses so many new components that it becomes more than just an evolution. The turbos, for example, are now much bigger and, to avoid the chronic lag that would normally result, exhaust gases are fed through two of them below 3,800rpm, after which the other two join the party. There's a new, beefier crankshaft, but it's no heavier than before and the con rods are also stronger but weigh the same. No fewer than 11 radiators help cool the beast.

The car's structure is more remarkable still: its chassis is made of carbon fibre with a layer of aluminium honeycomb in its core, and the body panels are all carbon, too. Engineers talk in terms of torsional rigidity, and Wallace tells me the Chiron is as stiff as a Le Mans Prototype One World Endurance racing car. This probably explains at least some of those strange sensations (and also accounts for, oh, about £1 million ($1.2 million) of the £2.5 million ($3 million) cost of the car).

It would be a shame if the Chiron's oily bits and colossal numbers overwhelmed its status as a design object. The project was overseen by the talented Achim Anscheidt, who has somehow reconciled aesthetics with the extreme aerodynamics that govern a car like this. The big 'C' on the Chiron's body side

is clever and the spine line directly references the Thirties Type 57 Atlantic (if you're going to pay homage to something, it might as well be this – just ask Ralph Lauren). The interior is the work of a young Frenchman called Etienne Salome, who maxed out on the material quality while ensuring the Chiron's cabin is future-proofed. So forget about central touch screens and apps that will order next Tuesday's lunch and revel instead in milled aluminium indicator stalks and a level of detail so obsessive the audio volume controls on the steering wheel are specially coated and the button for the interior light is trimmed in leather. 'I even enquired about removing the airbag logo on the steering wheel,' Salome tells me.

His efforts reward you even as you crawl through London's streets. The quality is immense, the experience all-consuming. A car this powerful shouldn't be so absurdly docile, as it shows lesser pretenders in Knightsbridge how it's done. Sure, you don't want to kiss any kerbs (the wheels and tyres are very, very valuable) and God help you if you chance upon any of the capital's notorious width restrictors. But the seven-speed, dual-clutch transmission is as smooth at walking speed as it is at 200mph, despite having to harness the same amount of torque as an 18-wheeler. Or a jumbo jet. It is, in every sense, astonishing.

The Chiron also goes round corners more smoothly and satisfyingly than the Veyron ever did and sheds its vast speed with the same savage implacability with which it accelerates. Does any of this really matter to the 500 people who'll actually end up owning a Chiron? Probably not. They'll be too busy enjoying the ultimate statement car, one that does its best work, paradoxically, at precisely 0mph.

Mercedes-AMG Project One
Winning streak

The competition heated up as Formula One leviathan Mercedes-AMG unleashed its track tech on civilian roads with a champion hypercar: Project One.

ENGINE
1.6-litre V6 turbo, 1,134bhp
PERFORMANCE
0–125mph in 6 secs;
top speed 218mph
YEAR OF RELEASE
2017
PRICE ON RELEASE
£2 million ($2.72 million)

Formula One's relationship with road cars has always been tenuous, no matter how enthusiastically engineers talk about 'technological trickle-down'. But the current V6 turbo hybrid era is different and it's a formula with which Mercedes-AMG has enjoyed spectacular success – at the time of writing, 64 victories out of 75 Grands Prix contested since the rule change in 2014. That's not winning, that's annihilation.

The Silver Arrows have never looked shinier, but now comes the ultimate track-to-road doozy: the AMG Project One concept. This, ladies and gentlemen, genuinely is an F1 car for the road – a projectile that transplants the heart and hardware from Lewis Hamilton's weekend wheels into a machine that can be driven by anyone, on any public road, in any weather (it has all-wheel drive and traction control). Perhaps they should call it 'The Unicorn'.

If we accept F1 as the tech trailblazer it is, then Project One hits all the right notes. This thing harnesses a 1.6-litre V6 turbo, four electric motors and all manner of voodoo to deliver a grand total of 1,134bhp in full-assault over-boost mode. Crucially, AMG's engineers are gunning for an overall weight of around 1,200kg (2,645lb), which promotes the 'power-to-weight' ratio. So we're talking about 1,000bhp per tonne. This, more than a 218mph top speed or 0–125mph in six seconds, is what makes Project One an event.

OK, it doesn't look as nuts as Aston Martin's Valkyrie, but the ambition is stratospheric. Mercedes-AMG F1 engine supremo Andy Cowell confirmed to *GQ* that Project One can idle happily at 1,000rpm, but revs to 11,000rpm (no road car has ever gone that high); it will start on the button every time; and the engine can run to 31,000 miles (50,000km) before it'll need a major rebuild.

The chassis uses a carbon-fibre tub with the engine as a 'stressed member', and the suspension is an adjustable multi-link setup, using competition-style pushrods and spring-and-damper units instead of anti-roll bars. This is all ultra high-end racing tech redeployed in a car designed to meander in Mayfair. Indeed, it can do the meandering without troubling the London congestion charge: Project One is capable of 20 miles on epower alone. Electrification isn't just part of the marketing spiel here; it also protects the engine's internals from self-destruction at low speeds. Just like the F1 car, this is a triumph of integration as well as engineering and imagination. Oh, and thermal efficiency.

Naturally, the path ahead isn't wholly smooth. An F1 engine is kind of...noisy, an issue the drivers deal with via ear plugs. Mercedes CEO Dieter Zetsche tells *GQ* he has yet to drive a prototype and won't until the interior noise level is sorted. 'It's currently running at about 125dB,' he notes wryly.

'He said that?' AMG boss Tobias Moers counters. 'It's loud, but not that loud...' Aural drama of this magnitude won't bother prospective Project One owners. Just 275 have been selected by Merc's top brass and they'll each be paying £2 million ($2.72 million) plus local taxes for the privilege. You can't put a price on authenticity or experience.

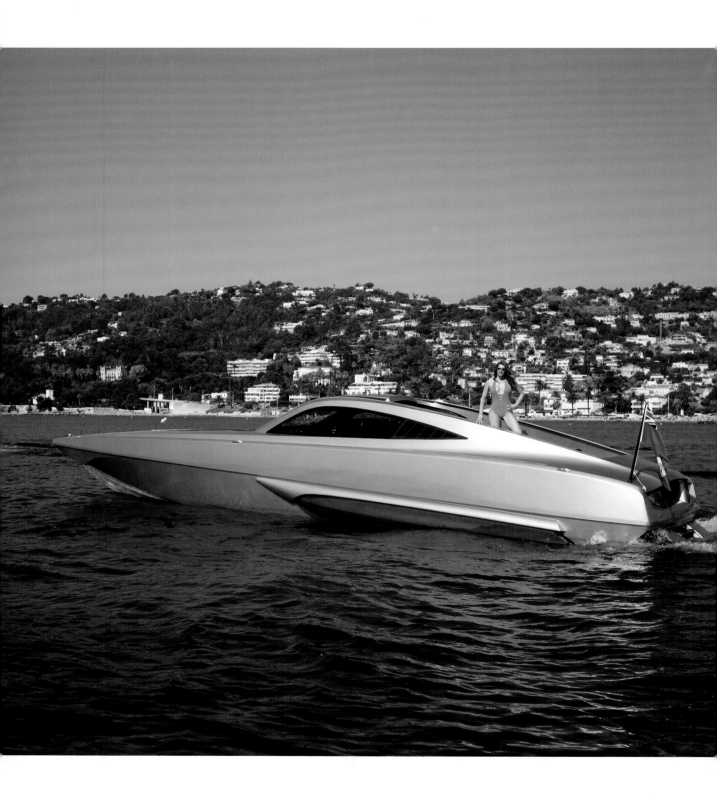

XSR48 Superboat
Ship shape

The XSR48 Superboat by XSMG was the first supercar of the seas. So, who better to dip her toe in the Monaco water than GQ's maiden voyager, Celia Walden?

The only piece of dating advice my father ever gave me was this: 'Never get into a car with an Italian male.'

As soon as I wasn't old enough, I did just that. The sense of abject horror as we sped the wrong way down a one-way street was only paralleled by the realization, a few minutes earlier, that Alessandro appeared to be wearing a fluorescent O'Neill 'fanny pack'. There and then, I made a vow to avoid near-death experiences and anything approximating 'surf clothing' for the remainder of my days.

All this comes back to me as a G-force sends the skin on my face rippling backwards into my hairline, and I lose control of my voice, tear ducts and dignity. I am aboard the new XSR48 Marine Superboat, billed as 'the world's first supercar on water', built in Britain by XSMG, but rather more at home in the Mediterranean. Which is exactly where we're 'driving' at a speed of 70 knots (around 80mph), having boarded in Monaco harbour, then zoomed off into the choppier waters of Antibes.

Simon, the multiple world record-holding test driver who refuses (worryingly) to give his surname but is in charge of this funfair ride, cackles loudly over the noise of the engine whenever he looks at me. Attempts at verbal abuse fail, as my expletives carry off pathetically into the wind. 'I'm not here to scare you,' he shouts. 'Sit back: you'll find it more comfortable.'

If I squash myself against the black leather seats any further, I fear I may have to be scraped off in a paper-thin cartoon state with a spatula. 'Let's be clear, this boat is for serious adrenaline junkies,' Simon says, as we slow down. 'Besides which, how else are you going to breakfast in Monaco, have lunch in St Tropez's Club 55 and be back in Monaco in time for after-dinner drinks at the Sass Bar?'

The guy has a point: it's one of those enduring dilemmas of the, 'Where are all the baby pigeons?' and 'Why do all women with corkscrew curls have very large breasts?' variety.

ENGINE
2 x 11.3-litre twin-turbos, 1,600bhp
PERFORMANCE
Top speed 70–80 knots (80mph+)
YEAR OF RELEASE
2006
PRICE ON RELEASE
£1.25 million ($2.15 million)

'For someone who has it all,' he surmises, 'this is the ultimate toy.' Only we're not talking Hamleys or FAO Schwarz here. The 14.6-m (48-ft) XSR48 – with its twin-turbo diesel engines (delivering 1,600bhp) and F1 technology – will set you back £1.25 million ($2.15 million).

Built from a lightweight carbon composite material designed for speed, the boat's hydrodynamic shape draws glances in a principality used to the parading of beautiful and expensive baubles. Designed to order, with only three currently in existence and four being built, the XSR48 has a handcrafted aluminium console, four to six seats in the cockpit and a double-berthed cabin beneath a glass roof, which boasts a shower room, leather sofas, an entertainment system – and the large, chilled bottle of Laurent Perrier I spotted earlier.

'The front cabin was designed more for a couple to enjoy themselves after a long lunch than somewhere to sleep,' chuckles XSMG Marine chief executive Ian Sanderson.

The windscreen can take 5 tonnes of water and be rendered bulletproof (for Russian buyers, I assume), although 'that does slow it down by about three knots', adds Simon – perversely making you an easier target. Oh, and if you're in the habit of having conscience-related issues, this superboat is not for you. The XSR48 uses a gluttonish 2.5 litres (0.6 gallons) of fuel per mile, making it about as ecologically sound as lighting a fire under an iceberg.

It's hot when you're in the driving seat ('There is no air-con,' explains Simon, 'It drains too much power from the engine') and the controls are complicated to use. Stabbing at the buttons marked 'trim tabs', 'blowers', 'horn' and 'screen' is inadvisable, says Simon, just as I begin to enjoy myself. 'If you sell this boat to the wrong kind of person, they could get themselves into real trouble, so there's a two-week training scheme before you are even allowed to buy it.'

Perhaps to illustrate his point, Simon cranks up the pace again. 'I'm going to do something very illegal,' he hollers, as we do a 360-degree turn and career off in the direction of Monaco Bay. 'Guess what the speed limit here is?' I attempt a nonchalant shrug, mainly because my face is too surgically tightened to speak.

'Twenty,' he says, laughing maniacally. 'And we're basically doing a mile in three to four seconds.' I'm starting to seriously dislike Simon. The boat comes clean out of the water for one or two seconds at a time, flying through the air like a dolphin on amphetamines, but mysteriously the XSR48 retains a feeling of stability.

'What? No noise, Celia? Feel free to scream,' sneers Simon. 'You have to know Celia very well before you hear her scream,' comes a voice from the back seat: *GO*'s photographer, revived from his paralysed state by the opportunity to inject a bit of smut into proceedings.

Sanderson is right to describe the XSR48's clientele as 'seriously wealthy and brave' with 'the posing factor as a key draw'. For 50 per cent of buyers, he says, this is their first boat, although 'all the people who have commissioned the XSMG Marine so far already own a private jet and a collection of sports cars'.

'You know what?' he laughs. 'One Russian owner even calls it his masterpiece.'

Chapter 9
Classic Cars

While most of the vehicles in this book were born in the 21st century, we reserved one chapter for a few unashamedly old-school rides that give classic cars a good name. As you will see, however, they aren't what you would describe as completely original. The beauty of these vintage Porsches, Jags and Mercs is that they have been given a new lease of life with some modern engineering touches, while retaining their original and timeless good looks. Of course, such makeovers don't come cheap, but if you were driving something that Enzo Ferrari described as 'the most beautiful car ever made', for instance, surely you wouldn't begrudge paying for a few mechanical upgrades? And as for the Aston Martin DB5, as driven by James Bond in *Goldfinger* (1964), that may or may not have had a few optional extras tucked away...but we have been sworn to secrecy.

Singer Porsche
Turn it up to 911

Meet the rock-star British Porsche enthusiast who cranked the classics all the way up. From retuned engines to full-body makeovers, we sing the praises of the mother of all restomods.

ENGINE
4.0-litre flat six, 390bhp
PERFORMANCE
0–62mph in 3.3 secs
YEAR OF RELEASE
2017
PRICE ON RELEASE
$600,000 (£487,000)

Like everything else in 2017, modern high-performance cars dish up instant gratification. Dual-clutch semi-automatic transmissions shuffle gear ratios so fast you hardly notice, carbon-ceramic brakes haul you down in mere seconds from speeds that were impossible a generation ago and a combination of high-tech rubber and chassis electronics generate cornering speeds that could dislodge eyeballs. But what price progress?

Singer's answer delivers a different, vastly more enriching sort of instant gratification. The car you see here has a 4.0-litre flat-six engine and, crucially, it's air-cooled, the way old Porsche units were traditionally configured until the late Nineties. It's good for almost 400bhp, and in a car that weighs around 1,250kg (1.4 tonnes), that means it's very far from slow.

But the key here is that you simply don't need to be going very fast before your nervous system is flooded with an intense mix of endorphins, adrenaline and dopamine. In fact, you don't even have to be moving at all: turn the key and there's that familiar Porsche rumble from the back end of the car as the engine catches, before settling into a thrumming beat. Brian Wilson wasn't the only person whose psyche latched onto good vibrations. Porsche's engineers knew all about them as well, especially above 4,000rpm.

It isn't just the car that's suffused with musicality. Singer's back story revolves around an LA-based English expat called Rob Dickinson, whose car-obsessed youth saw him graduate with a top automotive design degree and get a job at Lotus, before following the siren call of music. He did better than most (if not quite as well as his cousin Bruce, Iron Maiden's sandpaper-voiced vocalist). As frontman with Nineties post-shoegazers Catherine Wheel, Dickinson made five albums for major labels and ended up semi-retired in Hollywood with a hot-rodded Porsche, a personal passion project based on a 1969 911. 'I lost track of the number of people who stopped me to talk about it,' he recalls of his Sunset Strip showstopper. 'So pretty soon I figured that there might be something bigger in it. That's where the idea for Singer originated.'

These guys have become trailblazers for the restomod scene, a vibrant spin-off of the SoCal custom subculture where new components are blended with old-school aesthetics. Singer starts with its client's late-Eighties/early Nineties 911, before stripping the thing right down and beginning the sort of restoration that borders on the pathological, even in the frequently lunatic world of

high-end historic cars. The immaculately nuanced Seventies-mimicking body is made almost entirely of carbon fibre (only the doors are steel) and everything else – suspension, steering, interior, wheels – is completely bespoke.

The engine's crankshaft, oil pump, pistons, cylinder heads, throttle bodies, intake and exhaust are all new or reworked, Singer's team in the San Fernando Valley collaborating with LA's 911 go-to man, Ed Pink. All in, about 4,100 man-hours across 18 months are expended on Singer's 911 reanimation, and if you're thinking 'probably not cheap', you'd be right. On top of the donor car's cost, entry to this world starts at $395,000. Well, what else are you going to spend it on?

Except that with an estimated 18 million personalization permutations, including a dazzling array of interior options such as a rev counter that goes up to a Spinal Tap-referencing 11, that figure quickly ratchets up even further and the car *GQ* finds itself in – which is the only all-wheel drive the company has produced out of the 50 projects it has so far completed – ticks pretty much every box on its way to, gulp, $600,000. Each car is known only by the name of the area it's bound for, including Connecticut, Montreal and Manchester.

We're driving the 'Moscow' commission in Verona. The man who owns it likes to ski, hence the roof rack, also designed and manufactured by Singer. Ruinous for its aerodynamics, it somehow elevates the car to an even higher level. Maybe the owner's also a fan of the Robert Redford film *Downhill Racer* (1969), in which Redford's character drives, yep, a 911.

Piloting a well-heeled Muscovite's $600,000 one-off Porsche should rein me in, but the car's as generous as its owner's offer to drive it. Pretty soon, we're carving our way up and down this road at a fairly serious lick, and as it's running soft-compound winter tyres, it's not shy about sliding sideways out of second- and third-gear hairpins. But it's beautifully progressive, delicate and has arguably the purest steering feel of anything I've ever driven. Later today, the man who commissioned this jewel will be pointing it north towards Zurich or heading south to Rome. Wherever he goes, he's in for the drive of his life.

Icon Derelict
Revenge of the rust belt

*Call it the ultimate breakdown service...
we met the California re-mod studio making
new icons of individuality from husks
of American mass production.*

By mixing unrestored body panels with the very latest technology, Derelict cars have become their own trend that's still hot from the oven, bubbling with interest from Wall Street, Silicon Valley and some of the most influential minds in fashion. They're the antithesis of cars as an investment class and are, hands down, the most contrarily rewarding vehicle you can own in the world right now.

They're made by Icon, a company based in Chatsworth, Los Angeles – a neighbourhood that's home to a cul-de-sac of mortician-grey low rises. The brand built its reputation here by recycling and re-imagining vintage Toyota Land Cruisers with modern mechanicals and upgraded interiors, but its owner and CEO, Jonathan Ward, found that the concept of 'restomods' had its limitations: 'I dreaded the first scratch,' he says. The Derelicts are his response – cars with 21st-century driveability and a vintage aesthetic that gets better as it gets worse.

It sounds simple enough: find a car in a barn and stuff in a new engine. But underestimate their complexity at your peril – Icon's engineering team goes to extraordinary lengths to make it look like it did nothing. Like every Derelict that passes through Icon, a 1946 Oldsmobile Business Coupe was sent straight to a laser scanner before a single spanner was turned. That data was used to create a 3-D wireframe, then all of the modern elements – performance mechanicals, digital audio, climate control – were slotted into vacant nooks to optimize everything from connectivity to weight distribution. Clever stuff.

The depth of consideration goes well beyond the packaging and into the minutiae, so everything you can touch is high-functioning sculpture. The owner of the '46, a senior engineer at Apple, had a very specific vision for the final texture of his car that went right down to the knobs of the air-conditioning switch – it had to click when you turned it, a problem that took £5,000 ($6,250) of R&D to solve. 'Business-wise, [this work] is the dumbest thing we do, but it's also why we get noticed,' says Ward.

Icon lists among its customers one of J Crew's lead designers, Wall Street's money management community, foreign royalty and 'at least two' heads of state. But whatever they do for a living, they'll need to do it well because a Derelict isn't cheap. Prices start at $250,000 (£200,500), but the 1946 car set its owner back $350,000 (£280,000), and Ward says they can 'comfortably' hit $1 million (£800,000). 'We get celebrities and ball players too, but they're still buying Ferraris and Lambos for the most part.'

Yet, for the tastemakers, these cars don't so much stimulate an erogenous zone as define it. They're exemplars of postmodern luxury, prizing integrity and individuality above anything else. In the same way that a Rolex Submariner with a faded bezel is worth more than a restored original, each of these cars' individual patina can't be replicated, which gives it a value comfortably beyond the sum of its parts. Buy a supercar and it says precisely nothing about you, apart from the size of your wallet. The Derelicts are more reflective, more emotionally subtle.

Not any old rusting hulk makes the cut, though. 'The client almost never supplies the car,' says Ward. Mostly, they come to Icon with a concept, from something relatively straightforward, such as matching a car to an art-deco home, to more abstract briefs. 'One client asked me to build a car that reminded them of their grandparents at Christmas time.' Once the idea's locked in, Ward uses a nationwide network of hunters – who variously include architects, petrol station technicians, farmers and UPS drivers – to find the right car. 'It could be anything, but I have to get excited by it, and it's the individual vehicle that mandates the vision of the build.'

Despite dealing in old things, Ward is fiercely progressive. 'We avoid building younger [post-1965], more clichéd cars like Ford Mustangs. We'd much rather create something that's already visually exciting and then let people pull back the layers to find more surprises.' His next project, for example, is a barn-found 1949 Mercury Eight that's had its oily, mechanical guts replaced with Tesla long-range batteries, regenerative brakes and a pair of electric motors that'll give it 800bhp – 100bhp more than the Model S it borrows parts from. 'It'll still look like a '49 Mercury inside and out when it's parked,' says Ward.

Regardless of the tech and practicality, the Derelicts make no objective sense – you could buy a supercar and an interesting classic for the price. But your very own cutting-edge antique that's impossible to re-create? That's every expression of luxury stitched into the same thing. No wonder they're selling faster than Icon can pull cars out of barns.

Mercedes-Benz 300 SL
Putting the mill in Mille Miglia

GQ took a Mercedez-Benz 300 SL worth
seven figures for a grand adventure in Italy's
most historic race.

ENGINE
3.0-litre, 6-cylinder,
212bhp
PERFORMANCE
0–62mph in 8.8 secs;
top speed 135mph
YEAR OF RELEASE
1954
PRICE ON RELEASE
£2,483 ($6,940)

Who would you choose as a co-pilot if you were embarking on a three-day,
1,000-mile odyssey into the heart of the planet's most effortlessly pretty country?

'Remember,' Bernd Mayländer, the safety car driver in Formula One, says to
me, 'this car is worth about £1 million ($1.28 million). Think about what you
are doing.'

Trust me, Bernd, the thinking never stopped. Especially when that Fiat Panda
hung an unexpected left...

The Mille Miglia is the self-styled 'most beautiful race in the world', an
unparalleled mix of automotive jewels and stunning scenery, not to mention
an emotionally supercharged demonstration of the ongoing love affair Italy
enjoys with its automotive heritage. It isn't meant to be a race at all, more
a regularity rally, but for at least a third of the 445 entrants the driving is
manifestly done through a gauzy red mist. Despite my co-driver's rep, the
prospect of carving *GQ*'s red Mercedes-Benz 300 SL 'Gullwing' through
the improvisational traffic of small-town Italy soon becomes second nature.
Some of the locals love the bravado. Others don't notice you're there until
they're inhaling your fumes. At least one gives us the internationally
recognized single-finger salute. It's a fair enough adjunct to the beautiful
borghi, *portici* and *chiaroscuri* of this sensational country.

Of course, the modern Mille Miglia isn't as crazy as the original. The first
race was held in 1927, dreamed up by aristocrats Count Aymo Maggi and
Franco Mazzotti, who were incensed that their hometown of Brescia had been
supplanted by Monza as the home of Italian motorsport. On 26 March 1927,
77 cars set off on a figure-of-eight blast from Brescia to Rome and back again.
There would be 23 more races before the fateful 1957 edition, when Ferrari
ace Alfonso de Portago lost control of his 335 S. He was killed, along with his
co-driver and nine spectators, a tragic accident that led the Vatican's newspaper
L'Osservatore Romano to denounce Enzo Ferrari as a latter-day Saturn.

The Mille Miglia was resurrected 20 years later and has blossomed into
one of the greatest car events of all, a hyper-analogue salute to the romance
of internal combustion as we prepare to hand over to autonomous electric
vehicles. Long may it last.

If pushed, I would nominate Sir Stirling Moss's elegant victory in the 1955 Mille Miglia as the greatest in motorsport history. He completed the race in ten hours, seven minutes, averaging 98mph and often reaching speeds of up to 180mph in his Mercedes 300 SLR. His co-driver, journalist Denis Jenkinson, had recced the route and repurposed a toilet roll and holder for pace notes. Jenkinson frequently found himself vomiting out of the car and even lost his famous round spectacles at one point. Fortunately, he had a spare pair.

'Winning the Mille Miglia was a more difficult challenge than Le Mans [24 Hours],' Moss told me when I interviewed him a few years ago. 'The stress on the car was much higher and you were racing on public roads. I could learn the Targa Florio [the Sicilian equivalent], but I couldn't for the Mille Miglia. You can't learn 1,000 miles. To be honest, it was the only race that frightened me, at least until the moment the flag fell.'

Moss's Mercedes teammate was Juan Manuel Fangio. He came second in 1955, finishing 32 minutes behind the British pair but, incredibly, he did the race alone. Mercedes had his 300 SLR, No 658, on display ahead of the 2018 race, a car of such significance that it would likely make £100 million ($1.28 million) if it were ever auctioned. Mercedes-Benz Classic manages its heritage expertly, with the Ben van Berkel-designed museum in Stuttgart the centrepiece to an operation that includes a startling nine-mile-long archive. Leveraging the past is an increasingly important part of the future.

The team is fielding ten 300 SLs in the Mille Miglia, the convoy to end all convoys. The road-going offshoot of Mercedes' early Fifties racing car, the Gullwing was created at the behest of the company's entrepreneurial US dealer Max Hoffman, who ordered 500 as a sop to the initially reluctant management. The rest is pretty much history; some believe the 300 SL to be the first 'supercar', a machine whose design, engineering and performance immediately made its rivals look antediluvian. That said, it's a model with a certain reputation, thanks to a tricky rear suspension setup that gives it officially interesting high-speed handling traits. Still, what could go wrong across 1,000 miles of chaotic Italy?

Following a team briefing – in Brescia's baroque Teatro Grande – Mayländer and I spend several hours annotating our hefty, four-volume route books; they use 'tulip' graphics to set out the directions on each stopwatch stage and are easy to follow. Not so the red bits. These are the time trials, the component most critical to your overall ranking. The cars trip a beam to start, then have to maintain a steady average speed over a set distance before tripping another beam at the end. There are more than 112 in total, and this is how the – usually Italian (the MM is comically partisan) – pros win, drawing pinpoint accuracy from their timing equipment.

The roll call of towns and cities we pass through stirs the soul: Roverbella, Ferrara, Cervia, San Marino, Orvieto, Arezzo, Lucca, Parma, Monza...There is no language more mellifluous than Italian, no population keener to share in the love of an old car. Italy's cloistered medieval towns are always a joy, but sampling them from the cockpit of a car such as the 300 SL, high-fiving the bystanders as you pass by, is a reproof to a world that's lost its bearings.

The car is peerless. Like most histories, you don't drive it so much as reach a *rapprochement*. You might be going quickly, but you can't rush anything: steering, changing gear and especially braking all need a sort of forceful gentleness. Once committed to a corner, you stay committed or pay the price. Mayländer and I bond. This is also useful over 1,000 miles. And though we finish 142nd (pretty good, out of 445), bringing the car home in one piece feels like the sweetest victory of all.

Jaguar E-Type Speedster
Reverting to type

It may be a vintage classic that's been lovingly restored, but there's nothing reconstructed about the Jaguar E-Type Speedster's raw sensuality.

ENGINE
4.7-litre, 310bhp
PERFORMANCE
0–62mph in under 5 secs; top speed 160mph+ (estimated)
YEAR OF RELEASE
2010
PRICE ON RELEASE
£600,000 ($973,000)

George Best smashed around Sixties London in his E-Type, pimping out his precious ride to blondes met on a night's carousing at Tramp, just to seal the deal. And in the rare event of that gap-toothed grin failing to work its magic, the legendary maroon coupé, lithe as the footballer himself and just as fearless out on the field, would always do the trick.

The Jaguar E-Type, you see, is probably the only car able to make a girl's knees buckle on sight – dubbed, for that reason, the 'Shaguar' by Austin Powers, and described by the great American journalist Henry N Manney as 'the greatest crumpet-catcher known to man'. Maybe it's the legendary Lothario associations and cartoon curves. Or maybe it's just that in a modern motoring world of sometimes suffocating ugliness, a car of such supreme beauty comes not just as a pleasure – but a blessed relief. There's only one problem: as with the majority of absurdly attractive men, vintage cars tend to lose their appeal the second you enter into any kind of interaction with them. You'll try to ignore the tinny motor, tolerate the dodgy brakes and pass off the doors not quite slamming shut as a quirk, but essentially, we're back to the age-old female dilemma: pleasure or dependability? And women, pragmatists masquerading as sensualists, invariably go for the latter.

With all that in mind, the opportunity to drive a 1960s E-Type Speedster, restored to modern standards, had me slack-jawed with anticipation. Only 72,000 of these iconic machines were produced between 1961 and 1974 as roadsters and coupés, and this is the one and only Speedster. Down I sped to Brookside Farm in East Sussex, home to Eagle Racing Ltd, a classic car company specializing in bespoke, 'remanufacture level' E-Types. Since 1982, the firm's owner Henry Pearman has devoted himself to achieving a world-class reputation for building the best-reconstituted vintage Jaguars in the world. It's a Priory clinic for E-Types, a place where the beautiful and burnt-out go to be reborn.

And there it is, snarling up at me. An outrageous, one-of-a-kind caricature of a motor. The E-Type Speedster is the kind of car you want to spread yourself across – only with something worthwhile beneath that snaking bonnet.

'We call it the J-Lo,' laughs designer Paul Brace, as he helps me climb into the car – no easy feat if you're grazing 6ft. 'E-Types used to be built along the same lines as Twiggy, so we upped the curves a bit.' It's no surprise, then, to hear that this particular car, priced somewhere in the region of £400,000 ($649,000), has been hand-built for a man. The American doctor in question has customized every last detail, from the quilted, heated sports seats to the aluminium dashboard typical of the period, and slightly elevated eye line.

'He thought it looked too gentle first time around,' explains Brace. 'So we hoisted up the cat's eyes to make it look more vicious.' Five thousand man-hours have been spent on this motor. Now, finally: it's ready to be driven.

The doors slam shut with a satisfyingly weighty crunch, and I'm off, panicked, at first, by the powerboat rumble the car makes. The Jaguar roar has always sounded animalistic – but this is something else entirely. 'He wanted it to be as noisy as possible,' shouts Brace over the din. 'It was one of the requirements.'

Reach 4,000 revs and the car barks – a crackling of the engine that sounds fantastic but sadly disappears the more the car is driven. Some might call it a bumpy ride; I call it a real ride. There's no roof, so you feel the road and the elements as strongly as you feel yourself driving the car. After all, true Jaguar enthusiasts want not just the carcass of their E-Types replicated, but for that vintage character to be there, too. The George Bests and George Harrisons of this world were visceral men, unafraid of a bit of roughing up. Only when it comes to the things that matter, like the brakes, you've got the best that modern technology has to offer. 'When you buy an Elizabethan house,' says Brace, 'it doesn't mean you want to be throwing sewage out of the windows.'

Despite its curves, the car is really light, weighing in at just 1,066kg (2,350lb). This goes some way to explain why the E-Type takes off the way it does – gliding easily up to 160mph. Add to that the neat, hard cornering to rival any modern-day supercar and you have yourself the female fantasy: the most seductive of players with all its wiring intact.

Know what Frank Sinatra said when he first saw the Jaguar E-type? 'I want one and I want one now.' I can relate.

Aston Martin DB5
Do be careful, 007

The wheels keep turning at Aston Martin HQ, but a classic never dies.

ENGINE
3,995cc, 6-cylinder, 282bhp
PERFORMANCE
0–62mph in 8.6 secs; top speed 142mph
YEAR OF RELEASE
1963
PRICE ON RELEASE
£4,175 ($12,775)

I'm not promiscuous when it comes to cars. Few women are. I'll have my head turned like the next man by a shapely rear end or an arresting set of headlights, but it won't make me ditch the old model for something younger, slicker, newer. Which explains why the Aston Martin DB5 had my heart from the first moment I clapped eyes on it.

My tastes aren't exactly niche: the DB5 has been dubbed 'the most famous car in the world', with Russian oligarchs and Middle Eastern princes battling at an RM Sotheby's auction sale over the ownership of the model used in the early Bond films. (Only 1,059 of these little beauties were produced between 1963 and 1966 and, thanks to its unique past, this particular car finally went for £2.6 million ($4.4 million). Of all the Astons James Bond drove over the years, it's the DB5 – introduced in *Goldfinger* (1964) over 50 years ago and back for 007's last outing in *Spectre* (2015) – which is most synonymous with traditional British style.

This car is a spy toy of the highest order. In *Skyfall* (2012), when Bond takes a life-threatened M down a London backstreet to the lock-up where he keeps his trusty DB5, to drive her to his childhood home in Scotland, the otherwise vocal cinema-goers (what is it about Bond films that demands audience participation?) were momentarily silenced. To be afforded a lingering look at a car so classic that replicas had to be made using a 3-D printer for the film's stunts was awe-inspiring enough. To be allowed to drive the DB5 is the stuff my dreams have long been made of.

Climbing into this hallowed vehicle brings you down to earth with, if not a bump, then at least a series of ungainly – certainly un-Bond-ladylike – bodily adjustments. Over the past half-decade, the human scale has changed. My legs are concertinaed beneath me on the exquisitely patinated blue leather seats, my knees pressed against my chest and my back tilted forward towards the windscreen.

There's elegance in juxtaposition, however, and the sparseness of techno-artillery on the dashboard is offset by that magnificent outsized wood-rimmed steering wheel. It's just as well: any smaller wheel would be dwarfed by the £27,000 ($35,000) worth of Bond villain-esque Stephen Webster jewellery I'm wearing.

Forget the conspicuous absence of gadgetry and electro-hydraulic steering aids; the DB5 is all about feel. Turn the key and the 3,995cc six-cylinder engine blazes into life with a solid declaration of intent. It's more of a wrought burble than the obnoxious fanfare of the Vantage or Rapide (drop it down a gear and you get a louder growl) – the automotive version of a Spitfire flying overhead.

Vintage cars can often be a case of 'don't meet your heroes', but the DB5 isn't a museum piece: it's a car to be used and enjoyed – but firmly within the context of its period. Back in the day, it would have driven like a supercar compared to, say, a Morris Minor. Nowadays, it's at its best driven at an idle speed. It's the languorous sashay of a beautiful woman walking through a restaurant, revelling in the glances she's attracting, not the violent bitch strut of a catwalk model. Still, you can comfortably drive the DB5 at motorway speeds without attracting anything but admiring looks. Some of the old models have been equipped with power steering over the years, but there's something about the un-modernized version that better connects you to the road, with every twist and turn felt through the wheel.

Take it to its top speed and the wind noise rises to a deafening level, whistling around the doors, but the heating and ventilation are impressive given the car's age. I can't keep my hands off the chrome-tipped gear stick (insert lubricious Bond-style quip here). A five-speed gearbox was unusual in the Sixties – as were the car's power windows – and it's hard not to imagine that you could flip back the tip of that stick, press a button and eject your passenger with a smirk.

Like every man who ever donned black tie, sitting behind the wheel of a silver birch DB5 does, for a split second, turn you into Bond – or, in my case, one of his sinister consorts. Although I'd feel reluctant to dabble with the DB5, replacing the original tyres wouldn't be a travesty. The cross-ply tyres used in the Sixties have a habit of 'tramlining' (picking up every inconsistency on the road), but a lot of DB5s have since been fitted with radial tyres to give the car a smoother drive.

Smooth and easy is what this car is all about. And all the better for it.

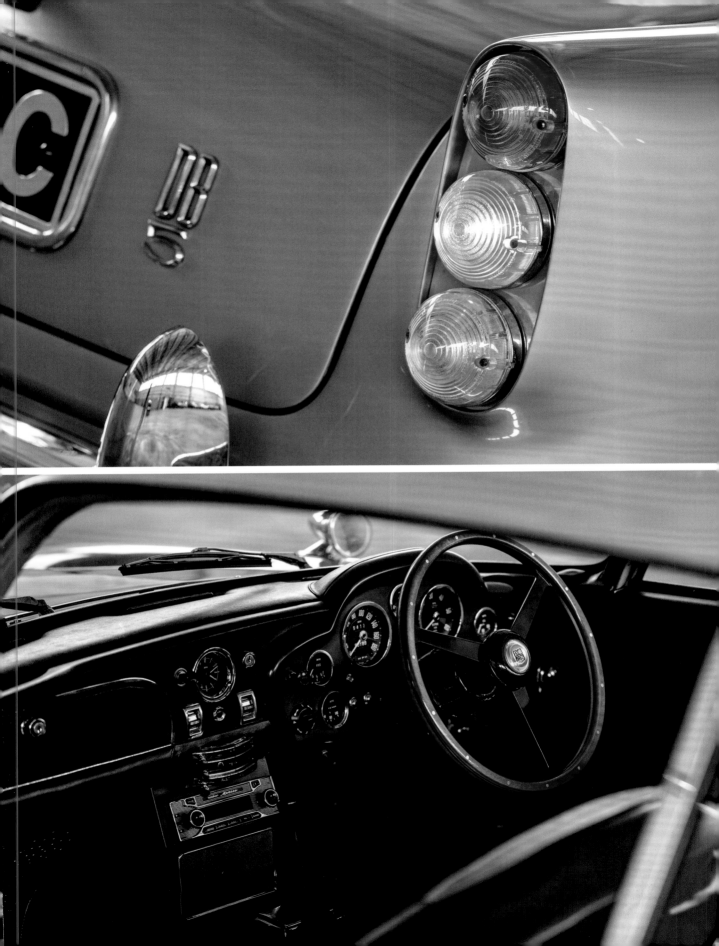

Mercedes-Benz 280SE
We can rebuild it

GQ's attempt at its very own restomod was a suitably stylish affair. Created to celebrate London Fashion Week, we created a car fit for a catwalk.

Anniversaries call for something special: a speech, a drink, a party. But rarely a classic car that looks like it's spent the last decade at the bottom of a canal. Yet, that's exactly how *GQ* chose to celebrate the fifth birthday of London Fashion Week Men's in June 2017.

The rationale was this: take an iconic car that could mix with the modern Mercedes-Benzes that ferry VIPs between shows, then give it some classic menswear credibility by adding bespoke touches not just inspired by fashion, but created by the very hands that shape it.

Enter creative director Patrick Grant and a 1972 Mercedes 280SE with most of its face missing. When *GQ* showed him how the car stood, he was surprisingly chipper about the eight-month time frame. He also had some ideas about how to drag it up to scratch. 'I think we should line it like a jacket. Something a bit different and a fabric that works in the city and countryside...silk.'

Grant turned to the silk weavers that supply his Savile Row house, Norton & Sons, and flipped through their old material swatches. He found a design from the same year the car was built, ran off a series of warps to match the black and green paintwork, then presented us with 3m (3½ yards) of material to work with.

Meanwhile, we made an addition to the suspension for reasons of aesthetic purity. We'd got hold of an original concept sketch of the Mercedes, as created by designer Paul Bracq, and there was no gap between the wheel and wheel arch. But by the time it was put into production in 1965, it'd been raised for real-world practicality. To get around the problem, Riiva Design had an Air Lift Performance setup installed. This allows you to adjust the ride height on the fly, so one minute it's low and sleek, just as Bracq intended, but when you arrive at an obstacle you can increase your clearance.

The silk and suspension paid tribute to the city, but the car's countryside credentials were looking a little thin. R Ward Gunmakers makes the finest shotguns on God's green earth and prides itself on its intricate, bespoke engraving work. We challenged the company's craftsmen to come up with an idea for the interior door handles to add some rural flair. The response? A stunning, hand-carved traditional scroll design achieved with only a microscope, a small hammer and a chisel.

ENGINE
3.5-litre V8, 200bhp
PERFORMANCE
0–62mph in 9.3 secs;
top speed 128mph
YEAR OF RELEASE
1970
PRICE ON RELEASE
£3,155 (estimated $12,000)

The car also needed something for the bit between the town and the country – travelling. So 120-year-old British luggage brand Globe-Trotter designed and built *GQ* a one-off 28-inch leather case, which swallowed our overnight kit, but also incorporated a concession to the car's age: a special compartment for some tools should we need to make any adjustments en route.

Insuring the thing was the next hurdle. Most brokers aren't geared up to handle bespoke cars built by the fashion industry's finest, but after several hours of furious googling, we found classic car specialist Heritage. It was able to cover the car so long as it wasn't raced. While the car packs 200bhp from its high-compression 3.5-litre V8, it's not the sort of thing you would ever want to hustle around Silverstone, so no problems there.

Then it broke. The Mercedes hadn't been on the road for the best part of a decade, so a few hiccups were inevitable. Luckily, the local Euro Car Parts store stocked most of what we needed (a water pump, battery and fixings), so we were on schedule for its final appointment: sign-off from Mercedes itself.

When *GQ* arrived at Mercedes' British HQ in Milton Keynes, there were several sharp intakes of breath. The technician responsible for the company's heritage fleet, Steve Constant, insisted the bumper was changed before it got the nod, calling on the manufacturer's peerless heritage department for spares. Job done. Now pass the spanners – we've got to get started on the ten-year project.

Index

Author's Acknowledgements

For Marilyn, Nyah & Fox.
Every journey has been better with you.

GQ Drives may have my name on it, but it wouldn't have been possible without a little help from my friends. Most notably, *GQ* editor-in-chief Dylan Jones for giving me free automotive rein within the pages of the magazine, but especially for the (ongoing) use of his company parking space. Thanks also to my car consigliere Bill 'Off-ramp to Hades' Prince, and to *GQ*'s Creative Director Paul Solomons and his talented art team, past and present: Andrew Diprose, Warren Jackson, Robin Key, Helen 'Twitters' Niland, James Mullinger, Lucy Watson and Keith Waterfield. And to the *GQ* subbing teams, past and present, without whom there would have been no big heads or hard sells: cheers to the chiefs Mark Russell, George Chesterton and AA-ron Callow.

Not all the images in *GQ Drives* were commissioned by us, but most of them were (usually the best ones) so props to our many photographers, including James Dimmock, Nick Wilson, Alex Howe, Jonathan Glynn-Smith and most of all to my motoring wingman Armand Attard, who made every trip an adventure, and every adventure a trip. I couldn't (and probably wouldn't) have done it without you, old friend.

Full Condé Nast respect to Harriet Wilson (and team) for all her continued support (three books and counting), and to Carole Dumoulin for her tireless research in the *GQ* archive.

Thanks also to Julian Alexander, and Ben Clark of The Soho Agency, and to the Octopus Publishing squad – Joe Cottington, Jonathan Christie, Sybella Stephens and Jack Storey – who helped bring this idea back to life and make sense of 15-years-worth of luxury wheel-to-wheel action. Big love to *GQ*'s contributing writers, from Boris Johnson and Nick Mason to Celia Walden, who generously offered to drive some of the most exciting cars in the world, and be paid for it.

And thanks, of course, to the one contributor I didn't have to pay. JB, aka Jenson Button, has been a friend of the magazine for almost as long as he has been a racing driver. A former F1 world champion and a *GQ* Man of the Year, I couldn't think of anyone better to write a foreword to this book (and luckily I didn't have to). Cheers Jens, and to his media right-hand man James Williamson.

Finally, to the other JB, a man without whom this book would not have been possible. Jason Barlow has been *GQ*'s car columnist for over 20 years and remains one of the magazine's best and longest-serving contributors. Not only is he the UK's top motoring journalist, he is also a great writer and a pleasure to edit. The majority of the stories in this book were written by him and I hope you enjoy them as much as I did when I came to revisit them. He may have questionable taste in clothes and an unhealthy interest in the Pet Shop Boys, but I love him all the same. Thanks, J'Blo.

An Hachette UK Company
www.hachette.co.uk

First published in Great Britain in 2019 by Mitchell Beazley, an imprint of Octopus Publishing Group Ltd
Carmelite House
50 Victoria Embankment
London EC4Y 0DZ
www.octopusbooks.co.uk

Text copyright © The Condé Nast Publications Ltd 2019

Design and layout copyright © Octopus Publishing Group Ltd 2019

Photography copyright © individual copyright holders All photographs courtesy of The Condé Nast Publications Ltd, except pages 38, 39 Culture Images GmbH/Alamy Stock Photo; 86 above & below Matthew Richardson/Alamy Stock Photo; 240 above & below, 243 above & below eaglegb.com.

Distributed in the US by Hachette Book Group
1290 Avenue of the Americas
4th and 5th Floors
New York, NY 10104

Distributed in Canada by Canadian Manda Group
664 Annette St., Toronto, Ontario,
Canada M6S 2C8

The right of The Condé Nast Publications Ltd to be identified as the author of this Work has been asserted in accordance with the Copyright, Designs and Patents Act 1988.

ISBN 978 1 78472 599 0

A CIP catalogue record for this book is available from the British Library.

Printed and bound in China
10 9 8 7 6 5 4 3 2 1

Contributors Jason Barlow, Domagoj Dukec, Patrick Grant, Dylan Jones, Matt Jones, Mark Lloyd, Nick Mason, Bill Prince and Celia Walden
Senior Commissioning Editor Joe Cottington
Senior Managing Editor Sybella Stephens
Creative Director Jonathan Christie
Designer Jack Storey
Design Untitled
Senior Production Controller Allison Gonsalves